LINGUISTICA EXTRANEA

Studia, 6

RECYCLING THE PRAGUE LINGUISTIC CIRCLE

Edited and translated with an introduction by
Marta K. Johnson

1978

KAROMA PUBLISHERS, INC.   ANN ARBOR

CONTENTS

INTRODUCTION

When in 1932, at the *First International Congress of Phonetic Sciences* in Amsterdam, the term *L'École de Prague* was used for the first time, six years had elapsed since the unofficial meeting of the group which later became known as the *Prague Linguistic Circle*.[1] On October 6, 1926 (considered the founding date of the Circle) a small gathering of linguists— Vilém Mathesius, Bohumil Trnka, Roman Jakobson, Bohuslav Havránek, Jan Rypka, and Henrik Becker— assembled to listen to an informal lecture by one of them, Becker, and decided to meet regularly thereafter.

Naturally, the linguistic activities of the individual members of the group began much before this date. In 1911, Vilém Mathesius delivered a lecture at the *Royal Czech Learned Society* [Královská česká společnost nauk] "On the Potentiality of the Phenomenon of Language"[2] in which he advocated a synchronic approach to language study five years before Saussure's *Cours de linguistique generale* was published and eleven years before it became widely known.

In 1911, however, Mathesius's approach to language did not draw much attention in a still largely Neogrammarian Prague. Mathesius had postulated a *linguistic characterology of language*— a descriptive method for establishing a hierarchy of means, idiosyncratic for each language, which the language utilizes in its communicative function. This characterology demonstrates the mutual dependence of language elements, i.e. the fact that no phenomenon in a language structure can be properly evaluated when isolated from the rest of the structure. Hence the term *structural* approach which the Prague School adopted as the method for its language investigation.

Just as the individual parts of a language depend on one another, so each element of the language as a whole exists only in relationship to specific extralinguistic conditions and has a function with respect to these conditions. This gave rise to the term *functional* approach, also intrinsic to the theory of the *Prague Linguistic Circle*.

It was precisely the structural and functional approach to language which served as the binding principle of the *Prague Linguistic Circle*. The range of individual interests of the scholars reached from purely Bohemian issues to general theoretical considerations. Specific issues were never discussed in terms of isolated theories, however, which would constitute an end in themselves. Every issue was analyzed as part of a larger totality within a specific linguistic and extralinguistic context.

In addition to the linguists listed above, there were many others associated directly or indirectly with the Circle. Perhaps the most prominent was Nikolaj S. Trubetzkoy, who, together with Roman Jakobson, made a permanent contribution to the study of *phonology*— a term coined by Trubetzkoy (originally in Czech, Russian, German, and French) for designating "that part of linguistics which deals with phonic phenomena from the viewpoint of their function in language."[3] The term *morphonology* (a shortened version of *morphophonology*—a domain dealing with the phonological structure of morpheme) was also created by Trubetzkoy and introduced in the Circle's *Manifesto*, read to an international audience at the *First Congress of Slavic Linguists* in Prague in 1929.

Questions of syntax, on the other hand, are most closely connected with Vilém Mathesius. His *functional sentence perspective* focuses on the communicative function of the sentence. The domain of poetic language and style was dominated by Jan Mukařovský, while questions of standardization of literary language were Bohuslav Havránek's area of study. Bohumil Trnka and Josef Vachek were concerned with general grammatical issues.[4]

Two periodical publications resulted from the Circle's activities— one internationally oriented— *Travaux du Cercle Linguistique de Prague* (1929-39), resurrected in 1964 (as *Travaux Linguistiques de Prague*), and one with predominantly Czech and Slovak orientation, *Slovo a slovesnost* [Word and Verbal Art] (1935-43, 1947–).

The present volume offers a selection of four works. The *Manifesto* appeared first in French in the introductory volume of *Travaux du Cercle Linguistique de Prague* (1929).[5] The other works were published in *Slovo a slovesnost*: the introductory essay to the journal (1935) and Ladislav Rieger's article (1941)— both in Czech, and Alexander Isačenko's article (1948), in Slovak.

The *Manifesto* was prepared by a specially appointed committee consisting of Jakobson, Mathesius, Havránek, and Mukařovský. The *Introduction* to *Slovo a slovesnost* is also a collective product of the members of the Circle: Jakobson, Mathesius, Havránek, Mukařovský, and Trnka. Rieger (not a member of the Circle) was inspired by the Circle's concept of structuralism while dealing with problems of semiotics. Isačenko was one of the earliest members of the Circle.

Chronologically, the four works represent the clearly formulated programmatic beginnings of the Circle, the further development and flourishing of its thought, the Circle's outreach and input into other disciplines, and the involuntary dissolution of its traditions.

The amazing variety of linguistic interest represented in the *Prague Linguistic Circle* is reflected in its *Manifesto*, presented as a programmatic outline of goals and methods to the *First International Congress of Slavic Philologists* held in Prague in 1929. The *Manifesto* did not appear in the proceedings of the congress, however— nor were the proceedings themselves published. Although the overall Slavic orientation is obvious throughout the document, the individual issues are placed within a general linguistic framework which clearly reflects the principles of the *Prague Linguistic Circle*.

The emphasis throughout the *Manifesto* is on viewing individual language phenomena not as isolated features but as parts of a system. This system, in turn, must be perceived and studied in a larger temporal-spatial-social context. Diachronic study is emphasized as an unavoidable complement of synchronic study, with comparative structural research providing the necessary broader perspective in time and space.

Special stress is placed on the function of individual language idioms in a social context and their relationship to extralinguistic reality. Gestures are viewed as the inseparable accompaniment of oral language manifestations. (Here, early attention to the issues of semiotics indicates a future focus.)

Standard literary language, in its role in lexicon development and language intellectualization, is seen not as a follower but as a leader. In its function as a tool of the ruling class in society, its evolution is marked by conscious efforts for reform and regulation. A contrasting effort to reach the widest stratum of the population characterizes its expansionist tendency.

Maintaining language stability and striving for its accuracy are the two principle goals of language cultivation. Elements alien to the character of a language should not be reinforced; on the contrary, efforts should be made to preserve and stress the individuality of the language.

The need for both synchronic and diachronic description is also considered necessary in poetic language, which is viewed as a distinct functional language, not to be equated with language in its direct communicative function. Because of the orientation of poetic language toward expression itself, all levels of its functional structure must be analyzed from a different perspective than in the case of a purely communicative idiom.

The *Manifesto* includes a section listing specific projects directed to Slavic linguistic investigation. These projects are diverse in focus but unified in the goal of improving each area of Slavic study. The *Manifesto* asserts that the position of Old Church Slavic in relation to older Slavic dialects should be reanalyzed. Both the phonetic and the phonological transcription alphabets should be unified for all Slavic languages. A comparative study is needed in the area of lingusitic geography— not only a purely linguistically oriented investigation, but one which would include considerations of social, political, and anthropogeographical character. An essential requirement for such an undertaking is an unbiased and equal treatment of all Slavic languages. Designing a general pan-Slavic lexical atlas based on a comparative study of individual Slavic lexicons is an inseparable part of this pan-Slavic project.

The last section of the *Manifesto* was added later. It deals with the practical problem of language instruction in the high schools, where linguistic theory is secondary and where emphasis should be placed on language practice. Instruction from the standpoint of a differentiation of function in varying language idioms is viewed as an essential requirement of a valuable language education, especially in one's native tongue. The practical character of instruction also ought to be primary in the area of second language acquisition. The details of instruction are determined by the goals which the individual types of schools are striving to achieve.

Although the linguistic principles of the *Prague Linguistic Circle* have not changed since the time of the *Manifesto*, a shift in focus became obvious six years later when the first issue of *Slovo a slovesnost* was published.

As in the *Manifesto*, language is here viewed as a functional entity within a larger extralinguistic context, but here the thrust is on the varying aspects of this context, on the relationship between language and the sense and purpose of its manifestations, between language and sign; that is, on semiotics.

A constant concern for the differentiation of language functions in different professions is also present both in the *Manifesto* and in the *Introduction*, but the focus of the latter is on the impact which these professions have on language and on their responsibility for correct sign utilization. Emphasis is on cooperation between linguists and various other professional groups, for only then can language responsibility and control be developed and maintained and problems of language cultivation resolved.

As in the *Manifesto*, the treatment of poetic language constitutes the essential and most comprehensive part of the program of *Slovo a slovesnost*. But here, though poetry is still viewed as a valuable tool in illuminating various language features (e.g. its sound structure), primary emphasis is placed on the study of language sign and its relationship to the structure and subject of the poetic work. Language study is vital from the standpoint of semiotics because the internal complexity of the structure of the sign is fully disclosed only in language. However, poetry forms a transition between language and other arts. Therefore art in general will also become a subject of research in *Slovo a slovesnost*. Even though seemingly remote from purely linguistic considerations, study of the personality of the poet and a study of the poet's relationship to society are inevitable, since language forms the relationship of sign to reality and both ends of this relationship must be analyzed.

As both the *Manifesto* and the *Introduction* were written by an almost identical group of scholars, one cannot argue that a generation change caused the shift in focal direction. This shift must not be perceived as a deviation from the principles of the Prague Linguistic Circle, but merely as the consequence of intellectual evolution— an almost predictable step in the development of the Circle's theory. In this sense, the *Manifesto* and the *Introduction* complement each other and a study of both is imperative for a complete and unbiased understanding of the Circle's intellectual tradition.

Rieger's treatise is an excellent example of the effect of the Circle's thought beyond its immediate boundaries, and of its inspirational potential.

Ladislav Rieger (1916-63) was a mathematician. He was the first in Czechoslovakia in his profession to work in the area of mathematical logic (specifically in Boolean and other abstract algebras).[6]

Rieger's article dates from the time when his teaching activity in the Department of Esthetics at Charles University in Prague was temporarily interrupted by World War II. Rieger's attention thus turned to other areas related to mathematics— philosophy, logic, and language.

Rieger was intrigued by the Circle's structuralist approach to language in that it did not view language as an aggregate of isolated features but as a constantly evolving, dynamic sign system.

As a point of departure, Rieger uses the theory of signs which Charles Morris developed in logic. It deals with sign relationships on three separate levels:

1. Formal relationships between signs (*logical syntax*): The syntactic level of interpretation is equated to algebraic and geometric formulae, which, once created, become independent entities wherein the result of their application does not depend on the user's comprehension of their details.

2. Relationship of the sign to what it designates (*semantic dimension*): The semantic interpretation abstracts signs from the context

in which they occur, as well as from their broader meaning.

3. Relationship of the sign to its user (*pragmatic dimension*): Meaning enters into sign utilization with the human element. Here, the behavioristic point of view is most frequently applied.

Rieger recognizes that a lingusitic semiotic study is far more complex than abstract relationships in logic, and thus Morris's formal model, though not to be completely ignored, is only acceptable for study of language-related issues on a limited basis. The main reason for Rieger's caveat is Morris's disregard of the temporal-spatial dimension, indispensable in an interpretation of human communication.

Rieger proceeds to point out that it is the interaction of the three levels of the relationship of the sign, above all the pragmatic dimension (the element of human mind) which adds the temporal-spatial component to the communicative act and which has to be included in subsequent interpretation. The importance of the effect of the human element can be seen in cases where the temporal-spatial dimension of the sign is reduced to only the temporal level (i.e. music), or where it is absent (moods, emotions), thus rendering a unique human experience almost non-communicable.

This element of the unique which caused non-communicability is particularly obvious in a translation-interpretation of philosophical texts where the direct temporal-spatial experience of both the translator and the interlocutor are by definition missing.

Rieger offers a thorough account of several texts selected from the works of classical Greek philosophers and translated into German. He then investigates those details of the interpretative process which would allow a rendering of the translations with the least distortion of the philosopher's original idea. He arrives at the conclusion that the only possible way to make a relatively correct interpretation is to approach as closely as possible the original situation in which the philosopher was creatively active. This can be done by investigating other (both philosophical and non-philosophical) texts produced by the same author in the identical temporal-spatial context where identical language elements occur. The social and intellectual position of the philosopher as innovator in his specific social context is also extremely important for the correct interpretation of his thought.

Semiotics, a discipline dealing with the sign, can account for an adequate interpretation of philosophical texts as long as it does not separate the three dimensions of interpretation and allows other relevant aspects of reality, both of a linguistic and of a non-linguistic nature, to enter into the interpretative process. The mathematical-logical model is hardly relevant in the area of semiotics because exact sciences require nothing more than flat models in the application of their formulae.

According to Rieger, the basic problem in an interpretation of philosophical texts is caused by the discrepancy between the richness of thought on the one hand, and by the language's striving for objectivization and generalization on the other— efforts which result in the language's inadequacy in rendering the unique.

Another problem has to be considered: The thought of a philosopher can be partially under his control, his property, only during his lifetime. But even then, and more so after his death, elements and interpretations foreign to the philosopher's way of thinking may enter the boundaries of his thought and distort it. This is especially true in a translation-interpretation, where the thought has to be rendered as closely as possible to the intent of the philosopher. On the other hand, the result of the translation has to be intelligible and relevant, both linguistically and ideologically, for its new audience, whose temporal-spatial context differs from that of the philosopher. The translator thus has to account for a dual temporal-spatial context and a dual linguistic context (and for the language evolution in between), while trying to remain in the philosopher's realm of thought. This is certainly not an easy task.

Whereas Rieger, an outsider, viewed language within a larger context of extralinguistic reality, fully in accord with the tradition of the *Prague Linguistic Circle*, Isačenko, a member of the Circle, distorted the Circle's principles, especially in the area of methodological approach.

His article thus foreshadows and at the same time symbolizes the end of the Circle's traditions.

Alexander Vasiljevič Isačenko (1911-78) was Trubetzkoy's
student in Vienna. He helped found the *Bratislava Linguistic Circle*
(1945-50) and served as its vice-president. He taught at the univer-
sities in Bratislava and Olomouc, and eventually became head of
the Slavic Section of the Institute of Languages in the Czechoslovak Academy of Science in Prague. Isačenko spent the last decade
of his life in Austria at the University of Klagenfurth.

The argument of Isačenko's article is that the sentence as a mini-
mal linguistic unit of predication ought to become the focal point
of linguistic investigation.

After rejecting the subject-predicate system as it is dealt with in
logic and refuting the Herbartian psychological concept of images,
Isačenko makes an *a priori* assertion that the two basic elements of
language are sentence and word. As words acquire meaning only in
sentences, Isačenko suggests a reanalysis of every concrete instance
of the word:sentence relationship which would then produce a
satisfactory definition of the word, specific for every language.

Discarding syntax as too vague a discipline, he arrives at the conclusion that only grammar is suitable for dealing with the sentence
as a linguistic unit. As every language form is demonstrated in a
sentence and as grammar is the domain of forms of language which
occur in the predicative function, grammar is actually identical
with sentence specific instruction.

Linguistic disciplines can then be divided into four categories: 1.
grammar, 2. *lexicon*, 3. *stylistics*, and 4. *phonology*. Lexicon (with
word-formation) is of a non-systemic nature. So, too, is stylistics,
which is the domain of all language formations that extend beyond a sentence frame (paragraph, utterance, as well as the entire
area of poetic language). Phonology is an independent domain of
linguistic investigation which partially penetrates each of the a-
bove disciplines (resulting in separate systems of lexical, grammatical, and stylistic phonology).

Grammar is the only domain of language research which is of a
systemic nature and within which language structures can be investigated. Only productive sentence types belong to grammar.
Solidified phrases (e.g. of a proverbial type) form part of another

discipline which Isačenko calls idiomatics. Besides productive sentence types, all formal categories applicable within a sentence framework (declensions, word-order, agreement, etc.) belong to grammar.

There are several points where Isačenko departs radically from the traditional teaching of the *Prague Linguistic Circle*. He reverses the hierarchy of linguistic investigation by negating the primacy of phonology, disregards the function of utterance as a valid tool in sentence analysis, and separates the contents of the individual linguistic disciplines. Isačenko's attitude to the form:meaning relationship is quite confusing and the role of extralinguistic reality is presented in very vague terms.

The article was written in a period that was strongly influenced by the teaching of Nikolai J. Marr, who had "paralyzed the greater part of linguistic (especially historical) research work" in the Soviet Union.[7] In 1950, Stalin put an end to the teaching of Marr's theories in the Soviet Union,[8] thereby instigating a broad linguistic debate within the country. That same year, Isačenko subjected Marr to severe criticism in Czechoslovakia.[9] He also criticized Ivan I. Meščaninov[10] whom he himself had introduced (and whose work he had supported before the Czechoslovak linguistic audience) in the article included in this volume.

Isačenko's attitude typifies the period in which his article appeared. It epitomizes the post-war situation in linguistic research and foreshadows the dissolution of the traditions which the *Prague Linguistic Circle* had developed in the two decades of its existence.

In the 1950s, new linguistic organizations replaced the *Prague Linguistic Circle*. The intellectual heritage of the Circle had, however, become international property long before that time. The Circle's ideas continued to be developed abroad, especially in the United States, without interruption. In the early sixties, the students of Trnka, Vachek, and others revived interest in the traditions of the *Prague Linguistic Circle* within Czechoslovakia. The success of this revival verifies the timeless quality and relevancy of the open-minded approach to linguistic problems which the *Prague Linguistic Circle* had advocated. It demonstrates that only an approach which places language within a larger socio-historical context can provide the necessary prerequisites for unbiased linguistic research.

I am grateful to Ladislav Matejka for his valuable help with the selection of the texts for translation. My thanks also go to Susan Stapleton, Paul Roberge, Herbert Eagle, and especially Owen V. Johnson, each of whom read and commented on individual sections.

Marta K. Johnson   Ann Arbor, Michigan
                                                     August, 1978

NOTES

1. Much has been written about the history and theory of the Prague Linguistic Circle. For detailed accounts, among others, see: Josef Vachek, *The Linguistic School of Prague* (Bloomington-London: Indiana University Press, 1966); Ladislav Matejka, ed., *Sound, Sign and Meaning: Quinquagenary of the Prague Linguistic Circle*, Michigan Slavic Contributions, No. 6 (Ann Arbor: Michigan Slavic Publications, 1976).

2. Vilém Mathesius, "O potenciálnosti jevů jazykových." In: *Věstník Královské české společnosti nauk*, třída filosoficko-historická, 1911. Translated into English by Josef Vachek and published in *A Prague School Reader in Linguistics* (Bloomington: Indiana University Press, 1964), pp. 1-32.

3. Vachek, *The Linguistic School of Prague*, p. 41.

4. For a more complete list, see: Vachek, *The Linguistic School of Prague*, pp. 122-136.

5. The present translation is based on the original Czech text which was printed in: *U základů pražské jazykovědné školy* [At the Foundation of the Prague Linguistic School], publ. by Josef Vachek (Prague: Academia, 1970), pp. 35-65.

6. For more information on Rieger, see his *Algebraic Methods of Mathematical Logic* (New York and London: Academic Press, 1967).

7. Vachek, *The Linguistic School of Prague*, p. 13.

8. For a more detailed account of this debate see: *The Soviet Linguistic Controversy*, transl. from the Soviet Press by John V. Murra, Robert M. Hankin, Fred Holling (New York: King's Crown Press, 1951); *Za marxistickú jazykovedu*, ed. by A. V. Isačenko (Bratislava: Slovenská akadémia vied a

umení, 1950).

9. A. V. Isacenko, "Hlavné črty Marrova učenia o jazyku." In:*Za marxistickú jazykovedu*, pp. 237-251.

10. *Za marxistickú jazykovedu*, p. 249.

MANIFESTO
PRESENTED TO THE FIRST CONGRESS OF SLAVIC PHILOLOGISTS IN PRAGUE 1929[1]

1. *Methodical problems resulting from the concept of language as a system and the importance of this concept for Slavic languages.* (The synchronic method and its relation to the diachronic method, structural vs. genetic comparison, incidental vs. natural order in the continuum of language development phenomena.)
a. The concept of language as a functional system.

Language and human activity, from which language results, share the element of intention. Whether language is analyzed as an expression or as information, the intention of the speaker is the easiest and most natural explanation. Therefore, the functional aspect ought to be considered in a linguistic analysis. From the functional standpoint, language is a system of instrumental means of expression. No language phenomenon can be understood without considering the system of which it is a part. Slavic linguistics cannot avoid facing this pertinent complex of problems.

b. Tasks of the synchronic method: its relationship to the diachronic method.

The substance and character of a language system is best perceived through a synchronic analysis of modern languages, because only these provide full material and can be directly experienced. The most urgent and also the most neglected task of Slavic linguistics is thus to outline linguistic characteristics of the modern Slavic languages. A deeper study of the Slavic languages is impossible without this prerequisite.

The concept of language as a functional system even applies in studying its older stages, both in their reconstruction and in surveying their evolution. It would be unreasonable to erect insurmountable barriers between the synchronic and the diachronic method as the Geneva school does. If the elements of language systems are to be evaluated in synchronic linguistics from the viewpoint of their functions, the changes in language cannot be judged while ignoring the system which is subject to these changes. It

would be illogical to assume that language changes are only inter-
ferences without purpose, heterogeneous from the viewpoint of
the system. Language changes frequently have an impact on the
system, on its stabilization, reconstruction, etc. Thus, diachronic
research not only does not exclude the phenomena of system and
function, but is, on the contrary, incomplete if it disregards them.

Conversely, a synchronic description cannot entirely ignore the
notion of evolution, because the idea of past, present, and future
stages is inherent even in synchronically examined periods; stylistic elements, experienced as archaisms, and the distinction between productive and unproductive forms constitute a proof of
diachronic phenomena which cannot be eliminated from synchronic linguistics.

c. New prospects for the application of the comparative method.

Thus far, the comparative research of Slavic languages has been
limited to genetic problems, above all to summarizing common
features. The comparative method has to be used on a broader
basis, however; it is a method concerned with the uncovering of
structural laws of language systems and their development. Not
only languages that are unrelated or related only distantly, differing structurally to the highest possible degree, constitute appropriate material for this type of comparison, but also languages belonging to one family belong here; e.g. Slavic languages which exhibit in their development sharp variances against a background of
numerous and substantial cases of conformity.

The consequences of structural comparison of related languages.

The comparative study of the step by step development of Slavic
languages is destroying the image of an incidental and episodic
character of the convergent and divergent development which
was manifested in the evolution of these languages. A comparative
study reveals a legitimate connection between the individual
convergent and divergent phenomena. This kind of research would
furnish a typology for the development of the Slavic languages,
e.g., a summary of a series of changes connected in a whole.

On the one hand, structural comparison provides valuable mater-

ial for general linguistics, and, on the other, enriches the individual
Slavic language histories. It definitely clears away the sterile and
fictive method of the history of isolated phenomena, uncovers
fundamental tendencies of one language or another and more substantially employs the principle of relative chronology, which is
more reliable than indirect chronological data drawn from documents.

Regional Groups

Uncovering tendencies in the development of the individual Slavic languages in different time periods and confronting these tendencies with the developmental tendencies in the neighboring languages, Slavic as well as non-Slavic (e.g. Finno-Ugric languages, German, Balkan languages of whatever origin), will provide material
for a set of important questions concerning regional groups of differing size, which the individual Slavic languages entered in the
course of their development.

d. The regular progression of developmental langauge phenomena.

In the developmental sciences, where historical linguistics belongs, the concept of an incidental occurrence of phenomena—
even when these are subsequently consistently implemented—gives
way to a regular progression of developmental phenomena (nemo-
genesis). Therefore, the theory of convergent development expresses the conception of a mechanical and incidental expansion
even in the analysis of grammatical and phonological changes.

1. *The consequences for an expansion of language features.*

The expansion of language features which change the language
system in question does not proceed in a mechanical way but is
determined by an aptitude for absorption, which manifests itself
in agreement with developmental tendencies. Thus, basic disagree-
ments over whether we are dealing with a change expanding from
one center or with a phenomenon resulting from convergent development will disappear.

2. *The consequences for the problem of the disintegration of proto-language.*

The sense of the problem of the disintegration of the proto-lang-

uage is thus changed. The criteria for the unity of the proto-language are the degrees to which the dialects are capable of under-
going common change. The problem whether these convergences
do or do not originate in one center is secondary and almost insoluble. As long as convergences predominate divergences, it is useful to presume a proto-language conventionally. Even the question
of the disintegration of the Slavic proto-language can be solved
from this standpoint. The notion of language unity used here is
naturally only a methodological auxilliary notion, designated for
historical research, and not suitable for applied linguistics, where
the criterion of language unity is specified by the relationship
of the speech community to the language, and not by objective
phenomena.

2. *The tasks of the research of a language system, particularly
Slavic.*
a. Research on the sound system.
The importance of the acoustic aspect.
The problem of the intentionality of phonological phenomena in
an investigation of the external aspect of these phenomena by definition leads to a primacy of their acoustical aspect in the research, since the speaker's concern is acoustic, not motoric (e.g.
various details of the articulation of the Czech [ř], Russian [l],
etc., are irrelevant when the acoustical result is identical).
*The necessity for a distinction between sound as an objective fact
in physics and as an image and an element of a functional system.*
An instrumental notation of objective acoustic and motoric provisions for subjective acoustic-motoric images is valuable as an index of objective correlatives of language values. These objective
provisions, however, have only an indirect relationship to linguistics and must not be identified with language values.
Even subjective acoustic motoric images, however, form elements
of a language system only to the degree to which they fulfill
the function of differentiation of meaning. The sensory content
of such phonological elements is less essential than their mutual
relations within the system (a structural principle of phonological

systems).

The Principle Tasks of Synchronic Phonology

1. It is necessary to characterize the phonological system, i.e. to determine the complex of elementary acoustic motoric images which form meaning in the given language (phonemes); while doing this, the relations between phonemes must be specified, i.e. the structural pattern of the given system must be determined; a delimitation of these differences in the phonological correlation which effect meaning is of particular importance. Phonological correlation is formed by a number of pairs of contrastive phonemes, distinctive according to an equal principle. This principle can be merely reflected, abstracted from each of the pairs (e.g. the following correlations exist in Russian: dynamic stress:unstressed vowels, voiced:voiceless consonants, soft:hard consonants; in Czech: long:short vowels, voiced:voiceless consonants).

2. It is necessary to determine the combinations of phonemes implemented in the particular language as contrasted against all theoretically possible combinations of these phonemes, the variations in their grouping and the extent of these combinations.

3. The degrees of utilization of these phonemic combinations, the density of implementation of these phonemes and their combinations must be determined; the functional load of different phonemes and phonemic combinations in the particular language must also be investigated.

4. An important problem in linguistics, particularly in Slavic linguistics, is the morphological utilization of phonological contrasts; i.e. morphophonology, or abbreviated, morphonology. Complex concepts of two or more phonemes, mutually replaceable within one and the same morpheme according to conditions of morphological structure of the word morpheme play a basic role in Slavic languages, e.g. in Russian $/k/$: $/\check{c}/$ is a morpheme in *ruk/č — ruka* 'hand', *ručnoj* 'manual'.

An exact synchronic determination of all morphemes in each Slavic language or dialect is necessary. It is also essential to determine the positions which a particular morphoneme can occupy within a morpheme.

An urgent problem in Slavic lingusitics is to carry out the indicated phonological and morphophonological description of all Slavic languages and their dialects.

b. Investigation of the word and word combinations.
The discipline of language denotation — word.

The word, from the viewpoint of function, is a result of a denotative function of language. This function is, at times, inseparably bound with the function of congruence. Linguistics, which analyzed speech as an objectivized mechanical fact, often denied the existence of word. From the functional standpoint, however, an independent existence of the word is quite obvious, even though its intensity differs from language to language and constitutes only a potential factor. Through this denotative function, speech segments reality, both internal and external, real and abstract, into elements appreciable by language.

Each language has its own denotative system: it uses different denotative forms with varying degrees of intensity, e.g. derivations, compounding of words, and stable word combinations (so in Slavic languages, particularly in the folk idiom, new nouns formed primarily by derivations). Each language has its own denotative classification and develops its own characteristic lexicon. Denotative classification is revealed above all in a system of word categories, whose extent, precision, and reciprocal relationship must be analyzed separately in each language. In addition, classificational differences occur within the individual word categories; e.g. a noun has categories of gender, animate/inanimate, number, degree of explicitness, etc.; a verb has categories of verbal gender, aspect, tense, etc.

The domain of denotation partially analyzes the same language phenomena as a traditional discipline, dealing with word formation and so-called syntax in the narrower sense (that which examines the significance of categories and forms of words). A functional concept, however, allows for a connection between separate phenomena, for a determination of the systems of individual languages and for explanations where older methods merely stated the facts, as in the function of tense forms in the Slavic languages. The character of vocabulary in a particular language is not sufficiently determined by an analysis of its denominative forms. To determine its characteristics, it is necessary to analyze the extent and average, certainty in the meaning of language denominations in general, and that of the individual denominational categories specifically. The conceptual sphere which is particularly represented in the analyzed vocabulary must be determined. The role of language effectiveness on the one hand, and that of the increased intellectualization of the language on the other, must be ascertained. The means of completion of the examined vocabulary (e.g. loan words and loan translations) must be analyzed. In short, one must analyze the phenomena of the so-called semantics.

The domain of congruence — word combination (syntax).

When a permanent combination is not at issue, word combination is a result of congruous activity, which naturally is sometimes represented in the form of a single word. This basic act of congruence and the equally intrinsic act of sentence formation is predication. Functional syntax therefore above all analyzes all types of predicates, while paying attention to the form and the function of the grammatical subject. This function is most clearly manifested in a comparison of the functional sentence perspective (theme and rheme) with the formal sentence perspective (grammatical subject and predicate); e.g. this comparison shows that the grammatical subject in Czech is not thematic to the same degree as is the case in French or English and that the functional sentence perspective in Czech, with its word-order non-mechanized in a theme and a rheme, makes it possible to clear away the discord between the theme and the grammatical subject, which other languages eliminate by different means, e.g. by the passive voice.

The functional concept makes it possible to recognize the mutual dependence of the individual syntactic forms (cf. the aforementioned connection between the thematic character of the grammatical subject and the development of passive predication) and in this way also recognize their systematic affiliation and concentrations.

Morphology (domain of word and word group form systems).

Word and word group forms resulting in the denotative and congruous language activity are grouped into systems of a formal character. These systems are analyzed by morphology, naturally in the broader sense of the word: not a discipline parallel to that of denotation and congruity (traditional word-formation, morphology, syntax), but one which cuts across both disciplines.

The tendencies which form the morphological systems have a two-pronged cohesive direction: 1. to retain in the formal system functionally differing forms which reveal the bearer of the common meaning, and 2. the forms of the bearers of different meaning, determined by an identical function. The force of these two efforts and the extent and organization of the systems governed by them must be determined individually for every language.

The force and the extent of the analytic and synthetic principles in the expression of the individual functions must be stated in the characteristics of morphological systems.

3. *The problems of studying languages with different functions, especially within the Slavic language group.*
a. On language function.

Language research requires a strict observance of a variety of language functions and of the ways these functions are implemented in any given case. To ignore these functions means a distortion and to a large degree even a fictionalization of both the synchronic and the diachronic characterization of a language. Both the phonological and the grammatical structure of the language and its lexical composition vary in accordance with these functions.

1. It is necessary to distinguish between the expressed (spoken) and the unexpressed (internal) language utterance. An expressed utterance is only a special case for the majority of speakers because language forms are more often used in thinking than in

speaking. Therefore, it is a mistake to generalize and overestimate the importance of the external sound aspect for a language and necessary to pay close attention to potential language phenomena.

2. Elements important for the characteristics of a language are the intellectual or the emotional input into a language utterance. Both of these aspects either encroach on each other, or one of them governs.

3. An intellectual spoken utterance first of all has social purpose (it is designated for communication with someone); an emotional utterance occasionally also has social purpose, i.e. to evoke certain emotions in the listener (an emotive utterance), or it is an emotional discharge which occurs without regard for the listener.

In the social function, one must distinguish an utterance according to its relationship to extralinguistic reality: it either has a communicative function (i.e. it is aimed at the object of the utterance), or a poetic function (i.e. directed at the utterance in and of itself). Two gravitational directions must be distinguished for a communicative utterance: 1. situational utterance, relying on completion via extralinguistic elements (practical utterance), 2. the utterance strives to form the most compact, complete, and accurate unit possible, where each word equals a term and each sentence equals a judgment (theoretical or formulative utterance).

It is desirable to investigate those forms of utterances where one function prevails, as well as those forms where several functions transpire; the principal question here is one concerning the differing operative hierarchy of functions.

Every functional language utterance has its own system of conventions— its own language (*"langue"*); therefore it is incorrect to equate one function with language (*"langue"*) and another function with functional speech (*"parole"*— in de Saussure's terminology), e.g. to identify the intellectual function with the language (*"langue"*) and the emotional with functional speech (*"parole"*), etc.

Modes of language manifestations are: 1.a. oral manifestation, where a further dividing aspect is the circumstance whether or not the listener sees the speaker; b. written manifestation; 2. discourse

with alternating interruptions (dialogue) and one-sided, uninter-
rupted speech (monologue). It is essential to determine which
modes and which functions can be combined and to what extent
this can be done.

It is necessary to examine gestures systematically that accom-
pany and complete oral manifestations during direct contact with
a listener; these are important for regional language groups.

5. A significant factor in language stratification is the relationship
between the participants of speech contact (the degree of their
social cohesion, professional, territorial, ancestral and family relations) and the speakers' affiliation with several collectives, manifested in the blend of language systems in urban idioms. Herein belong: the problem of languages serving the function of interdialec-
tal communication (the so-called "standard, colloquial languages"), special idioms, idioms adapted for contact with foreign
language environment, and the problem of urban language stratification.

Even in diachronic linguistics, attention has to be paid to the
mutually penetrating impact of these language formations; not
only the territorial impact, but also the influence of various functional idioms, various modes of language manifestation, and various group and unit idioms.

The study of this functional dialectology in Slavic languages has
not yet commenced. For instance, a more systematic analysis of
the means of emotional aspects of language is still lacking. A study
of urban idioms ought to be started promptly.

b. On standard literary language.

Political, socio-economic, and religious conditions constitute
only external factors in the formation of standard literary languages; they help explain why a literary language originated in a
particular dialect, and why it evolved and stabilized within a particular period of time; they do not explain, however, why it separated and how it differs from the popular idiom.

This differentiation can be observed beyond the conservative
character of literary language; first, even when a literary language
is often conservative in its grammatical and phonological system, it

is creative in its lexicon; secondly, it never represents merely a past stage of some local dialect.

The distinctiveness of a literary language is caused by its role, particularly by the heavier demands made on it in comparison with those made on a popular idiom; literary language reflects cultural and civilized aspects of life: the advances and results of scientific, philosophic-religious, socio-political, and administrative-legal thought. This task, together with its goal of providing technical information and formulation, increases and changes (intellectualizes) the lexicon of the standard literary language; the need to make statements concerning new realities that do not have any direct relationship to real life require a vocabulary which has not yet evolved in the popular idiom; also the need to make exact and complex statements about familiar things in real life leads to the creation of words as terms, expressions for logical abstractions, and to more precise definitions of logical categories by means of language.

This intellectualization of a literary language is also caused by the need to express the continuity and complexity of thoughts— reflected not only in the expressions for pertinent abstract concepts, but also by syntactic forms (e.g. perfecting the dependent clause by more precise formulas). The intellectualization of the literary language is, moreover, in increasing control (censorship) of the emotional elements (i.e. cultivation of euphemisms).

The more standardized and prescriptive character of the literary language is joined to a more attentive and demanding relationship with the language. Characteristic for the literary language are an increased functional utilization of grammatical and lexical elements; particuarly intensified lexicalization of word groups and a more precise delimitation of functions. This delimitation of function manifests itself in a greater precision and differentiation of expressive means and then in enriched social language forms (language etiquette).

The role of intentionality is intensified in the evolution of the standard literary language; this is manifested in various forms of language reform (especially purism), language policy, a more con-

sistent regard for the lingustic taste of a period (language aesthe-
tics in transformations pertinent to the time).

The characteristic features of a literary language are represented
mainly in coherent speech manifestations and especially in written
utterances. The written idiom exhibits great impact on the spoken
literary language.

The spoken literary language is less removed from colloquial
language, although the line of demarcation between the two is still
relatively clear. Continuous speech, particularly public addresses,
lectures, etc., is shifted further from the colloquial idiom. Utterances with a reciprocal interference (dialogue) are closer to colloquial language. A dialogue constitutes a scale of transitional
forms between the canonical forms of a literary language and
those of the colloquial idiom.

Characteristic of the literary language is, on the one hand, an ex-
pansionary effort, a striving to achieve the function of a "koine";
on the other hand, it is the effort to become a monopolistic symbol of the dominant social class. Both of these tendencies are manifested in the character of changes and in the preservation of the
phonological level of the language.

All of these properties of a literary language ought to be considered in a synchronic and a diachronic analysis of the Slavic literary languages. Their analysis ought neither to follow the model
of analysis of popular dialects nor should it be limited to an analysis of the external conditions of the life and evolution of the literary language.

c. On poetic language.

Poetic language has for a long time remained a neglected area of
linguistics. An intensive analysis of its essential problems has commenced only recently. The majority of the Slavic languages have
scarcely been studied from the perspective of their poetic functions. Literary historians touched upon these problems from time
to time, but as long as their methodological linguistic preparation
was insufficient, basic errors were inevitable. A successful investigation of the concrete facts of poetic language is impossible without clearing away these methodological errors.

1. The principles of a synchronic description of poetic language must be compiled while avoiding the recurring error of equating poetic language with the language of communication. From the synchronic standpoint, poetic language has a form of poetic expression (*parole*), i.e. the form of an individual creative act evaluated on the one hand against a background of present poetic tradition (poetic language — *langue*) and on the other against a background of the present communicative idiom. The mutual relationship between poetic language and these two language systems is very complex and multifaceted and ought to be examined carefully from both the synchronic and the diachronic points of view. A specific property of poetic language is the emphasis on the factor of struggle and change of form, where the character, direction, and proportion of this change differ sharply. For example, proximity of poetic expression to the language of communication is brought about by contrast with the prevailing poetic tradition; the mutual relationship between poetic expression and the language of communication, while at times distinct, is at other times not experienced at all.

2. The individual levels of poetic language (e.g. phonology, morphology) are so closely tied together that it is impossible to analyze one level while completely ignoring the others. Literary historians have frequently been guilty of this kind of approach. From this thesis it follows that poetic language aims at expression in and of itself and that all levels of a language system that have only an ancillary function in the communicative idiom acquire more or less independent values in the poetic language. Language means grouped on these levels—and the mutual relationship between the levels aiming toward automatization in the communicative idiom— aim toward realization in the poetic language.

The degree of implementation of various language elements differs in every specific poetic expression and in every particular poetic tradition; the specific hierarchy of poetic values is determined by this difference. It is natural that the relation of the poetic expression to the poetic language and to the communicative idiom differs in each case with regard to the individual elements.

A poetic work represents a functional structure and its individual elements cannot be understood when taken out of their totality. Objectively identical elements can acquire entirely different functions in different structures.

Poetic language can utilize even those acoustic, motoric, and graphic elements of a given langauge, elements which are not used in the phonological system or its graphic equivalent. Nevertheless, the relationship of the sound values of poetic language to the phonology of the communicative idiom is unquestionable, and only the phonological perspective is capable of revealing the principle of poetic sound structures. The following belong to the phonology of poetry: the degree to which the phonological inventory is used in comparison with its utilization in the communicative idiom, the principles governing the grouping of phonemes (especially in sandhi), the repetition of phonemic groups, rhythm, and melody.

A special hierarchy of values characterizes poetic language. Rhythm is the organizing principle and all other phonological principles of verse are closely connected with rhythm: melody, repetition of phonemes and groups of phonemes. Even the canonical devices of verse (rhyme, alliteration, etc.) result from the fusion of various phonological means with rhythm.

Neither the objective nor the subjective acoustic or motoric aspect can solve the problem of rhythmization; this can be done only by a phonological interpretation which distinguishes among the phonological basis of rhythm, concommitant extragrammatical features, and autonomous elements. It is only on a phonological basis that laws for comparative verse technique can be established. Two outwardly identical rhythmic structures belonging to two different languages can actually be distinct when they consist of elements which have different roles in their perspective phonological systems.

The parallelism of sound structures employed in verse rhythm, rhyme, etc. is one of the most effective means of implementing different language strata. The confrontation of similar sound structures emphasizes both the concord and the discord of the syntactic, morphological, and semantic structures. Not even rhyme is a mere abstract phonological fact; it reveals morphological structure even when similar morphemes are arranged paratactically (grammatical rhyme), and, conversely, when they are not. Rhyme is closely connected with syntax (with the way various elements in a word group are emphasized and arranged in the rhyme) and with the vocabulary (with the importance of the words emphasized by the rhyme, i.e. with the degree of their semantic proximity). Syntactic and rhythmic structures are closely interrelated, regardless of whether their boundaries coincide or not (enjambement). The autonomous value of both structures is emphasized in either case. Furthermore, the rhythmic and syntactic structures of a work of poetry are emphasized by rhythmic-syntactic stereotypes and by deviations from these stereotypes. Rhythmic syntactic figures have a characteristic intonation whose repetition creates a melodic impulse which alters the intonational relationships within the language. Autonomous values of the melodic and syntactic poetic structures are thus uncovered.

Poetic lexicon is employed in the same manner as the other levels of poetic language. It is reflected in either the existing poetic tradition or in the communicative idiom. Unusual words (neologisms, barbarisms, archaisms, etc.) are valuable from the poetic standpoint because they differ from the commonly used vocabulary of the communicative idiom in their sound effects. Commonly used words, as a result of frequent use, are not fully perceived but merely estimated in their sound composition; unusual words further enrich the semantic and stylistic variety of forms in the poetic lexicon. The morphological structure of the poetic lexicon is particularly operative in neologisms. Unusual individual words are significant, but also entire mutually interfering lexical environments which vitalize the lexical material by their interference are significant.

Syntax, because of its multiple association with the other levels of poetic language (rhythm, melody, semantics), provides ample opportunity for poetic implementation; syntactic elements that are only marginally utilized in the grammatical system of a particular language, e.g. word order, acquire an essential function in languages that have free word order.

3. The scholar must be mindful of egocentrism; that is, an analysis and evaluation of past or foreign poetics from the perspective of the specific poetic customs and artistic norms in which he himself was educated. An artistic phenomenon from the past can naturally endure or be revived as an effective component in a heterogeneous environment; it can become part of a new system of artistic values, but its function is such an event naturally changes, and the phenomenon itself is subject to pertinent alternations. The history of poetry should not project this phenomenon into the past in a transformed shape, but should restore it to its original function, connected with the system in which the phenomenon came into being. An explicit, inherent classification of special poetic functions, i.e. an index of poetic topoi, is necessary for every period.

4. Poetic word semantics, sentence semantics, and the semantics of compositional units comprise the least methodically investigated areas. Multiple functions filled with tropes and figures should be examined. Following tropes and figures, constructed as a form of the author's presentation, objective semantic elements projected into the artistic reality are among the least analyzed thematic structures. For example, metamorphosis is related to comparison, etc. The theme itself is a semantic compositional structure and the problems of thematic composition cannot be excluded from the analysis of poetic structure.

5. Problems of poetic language usually play a subordinate role in literary-historical research. The organizing feature by which art deviates from other semiological structures is, however, not concentration on what is being described, but on the sign itself. The operational mark of poetry is thus a focus on verbal expression. Sign dominates artistic system. The literary historian defies the hierarchy of values of the examined structure when, as the primary concern of his research, he does not consider the sign but what the sign stands for and when he analyzes the ideology of a work of literature as an autonomous quantity.

6. This inherent characteristic of the evolution of poetic lang-

uage in literary history is frequently confused with a cultural-historical, sociological, or psychological deviation, specifically with reference to heterogeneous phenomena. What must be investigated is the poetic language in and of itself, not the mysticism of casual relationships between heterogeneous systems.

The poetic utilization of various Slavic languages constitutes invaluable material for a comparative analysis, for divergent structural facts are here present against a background of numerous convergent facts. An urgent task is a comparative theory of rhythm and of the euphony of the Slavic languages, a comparative characterization of Slavic rhymes, etc.

4. *Current problems of Old Church Slavic.*
a. If Old Church Slavic (OCS) is to be perceived as a language used by the missionaries and their disciples for liturgical purposes and which subsequently (in the tenth and twelfth centuries) became the literary language of all Slavs who employed Slavic liturgy, OCS cannot, for methodological reasons, be identified as one of the historical Slavic languages and interpreted from the perspective of historical dialectology.

Artificial, amalgamated, and conventional elements should be expected in a language which was not initially designed for local use, but which derived from Greek literary tradition and subsequently acquired the function of a Slavic "koine." Therefore, the development of OCS must be interpreted in terms of the principles that govern the history of literary languages.
b. Study of OCS literary documents from the tenth through the twelfth centuries shows that several local schools of OCS were formed. From the standpoint of OCS as a literary language, we are not justified in acknowledging only one of these schools as the correct OCS idiom and regarding the others as deviations to be neglected. Local OCS schools (literary OCS dialects) have to be exposed via analysis of the norms which the scribes established for themselves from the tenth to the beginning of the twelfth century; these literary dialects should be carefully separated from the living Slavic dialects which accentuate past literary monuments as errors

and episodic deviations from the norm accepted by the scribe.

In addition to the southern Slavic schools and the Russian school that results from them, the remnants of the Czech school and its traces in the oldest Czech ecclesiastical documents also require careful examination within the framework of the history of OCS.

c. The important problem in the evaluation of the origin and composition of OCS, as well as for the history of the living Slavic languages, is to determine the particular Slavic dialects the missionaries used as the basis for the formation of the Slavic literary language. This dialect cannot be derived directly from any of the preserved dialects of the Slavic literary monuments; historical-comparative analysis of literary OCS documents and an analysis of both kinds of OCS script will have to be employed in this determination; a comparative analysis of the oldest data concerning both alphabets also helps clarify the original structure of the alphabet and its phonological value.

d. The term "Middle Church Slavic" is more suitably used in the study of the further fate of OCS in its different schools in the twelfth century when substantial morphophonological changes which had occurred in the individual languages up to that point where adopted as the norm.

e. A very urgent and thus far completely neglected task of Slavic linguistics is the scientific compilation of the history of OCS to the present day.

From the point of view of methodology, equally pressing and important problems for Slavic linguistics are the history of the OCS component in the national Slavic languages, particularly in Russian, and the study of the mutual relation between this component and the other elements in these languages. Church Slavic components in the Slavic literary languages should be examined from the viewpoint of their function in different time periods, and the question of their values should be solved according to the demands placed on literary language.

5. *The problem of the phonetic and phonological transcription of Slavic languages.*

The principle of phonetic transcription should be unified for all Slavic languages; that is, principles for the realization of different phonemes should be developed which reflect the phonological composition of the individual languages.

In the interest of the synchronic and diachronic analysis of Slavic languages and particularly of Slavic dialectology, an equally important task is determination of the principles of phonological transcription, i.e. principles for a written reproduction of the phonological composition of Slavic languages.

Principles for a combined phonetic and phonological transcription need to be determined as well.

Lack of a standardized phonological transcription impedes work on the phonological characterization of Slavic languages.

6. *Principles of linguistic geography, their application and relationship to ethnographic geography in the Slavic sector.*
a. Establishment of temporal and spatial boundaries is an essential prerequisite for linguistic geography (or history). However, this prerequisite must not in and of itself become an independent goal of the theory.

The spatial diffusion of language phenomena cannot be perceived as an anarchy of individual isoglosses. A comparison of isoglosses shows that several isoglosses can be combined as a whole and that a focus of expansion of a group of language innovations and the peripheral zones of this expansion can be established.

A study of contiguous isoglosses shows what kinds of language phenomena are necessary in a causal nexus.

Finally, a comparative study of isoglosses is a prerequisite for the basic problem of language ethnography; namely, a scientific classification of languages, i.e. a classification according to the most productive criteria.

b. If we limit our research to the phenomena of the language system, it can be said that even isolated isoglosses are actually fictive, because externally identical phenomena can be functionally heterogeneous while belonging to two different systems (e.g. an apparently identical /i/ has a different phonological value in different

Ukrainian dialects: where consonant softening occurs before $/i/ <$ $/o/$, $/i/$ and $/ï/$ are variants of one phoneme; where softening does not occur, they are two different phonemes).

c. As in language history, comparison with developmental phenomena of different origins is admissable; spatial diffusion of language phenomena can also be productively compared with other demarcations, above all anthropogeographic isolines (i.e. borders of economic and political-geographical facts and with the widening of borders of material and spiritual cultural phenomena) and isolines of physical geography (i.e. those of soil, flora, climate, and other geomorphological facts).

The specific conditions of this or that geographic unit must not be neglected; e.g. a comparison of linguistic geography with geomorphology, so productive in European conditions, plays a considerably lesser role in the East Slavic world than does a comparison with climactic isolines. A comparison of isoglosses with anthropogeographic isolines is possible from both the synchronic and the diachronic standpoints (with the data of historical geography, archeology, etc.), but synchrony and diachrony should not be mixed.

A comparison of heterogeneous systems can be productive only when we bear in mind that the compared systems are of equal value; should the category of mechanical causality be interposed between them and phenomena belonging to one system derived from those of the other, then synthetic grouping of these systems would be distorted and scientific synthesis would be mistaken for a flat, one-sided evaluation.

d. When mapping linguistic or ethnographic facts, one must keep in mind that the expansion of these facts is not identical with the genetic or phyletic relationships and that it frequently covers wider territory.

7. *The problems of a Pan-Slavic, particularly lexical, atlas.*

The Slavic languages are so closely related that the differences between two neighboring Slavic languages are frequently smaller than those between two neighboring dialects of one language, e.g.

Italian. Almost all Slavic languages are in geographical contact with one another. There is no geographical contiguity between the South Slavic and the North Slavic group, but each of these groups in and of itself constitutes a continuous geographic unit; the one extends from Venice to Thrace, the other from the Böhmerwald to the Pacific Ocean.

Such conditions in themselves promote the idea of a Pan-Slavic linguistic atlas; there is no doubt that such an atlas is needed. A study of the comparative-etymological lexicon is impossible without a precise determination of the diffusional isoglosses of individual lexical items. Miklosich's and Bernekr's dictionary lists all Slavic languages which attest reflexes of each particular Slavic lexical item. These data cannot, however, provide an exact conception of the diffusional pattern of a particular word; because, in reality, the boundaries of such diffusion always cut across one another. The dictionary does not indicate this aspect. A precise determination of the isolexemes within the Pan-Slavic framework can reveal new vistas in the history of all Slavic languages.

The practical realization of such a Pan-Slavic atlas is, needless to say, easier than that of a linguistic atlas for each Slavic language. For the composition of a Pan-Slavic atlas, fewer places can be only visited rather than investigated in detail as in the case of a special atlas of a single Slavic territory. Then, too, the number of items on a linguistic questionnaire would be smaller for the composition of a Pan-Slavic atlas than for individual atlases.

The work can be organized as follows: all Slavic academies would select suitable boards for the composition of the atlas; pertinent bodies of scientists would do so in those Slavic countries that have no academies. Representatives of all of these bodies would confer on the following:

> a. the density and layout of the location where material will be acquired (an approximately equal density of all of these locations is necessary; differing local conditions have to be taken into account);
> b. a unified phonetic transcription;
> c. the text of the questionnaire; that is, the kind of words

that ought to be recorded.

The program worked out in such a conference committee would be adopted by all pertinent academic bodies and its implementation would be required of each of them. Each Slavic nation would thus finance and organize acquisition of the dialect material on its territory according to the proposed plan. With regard to Slavic minorities within non-Slavic states, the proposed conference committee would have to establish contacts with the academies of the pertinent states in order to organize a linguistic-geographical study of these Slavic minorities in accordance with the proposed program.

Finally, publication of a Pan-Slavic linguistic atlas would be executed from the means furnished by all academies in the Slavic countries and under the auspices of a special committee established by the above-mentioned board of academies.

8. *Methodological problems of Slavic lexicography*.

The study of the origin of individual words and the changes in their meaning is necessary for general psychology, cultural history, and linguistics in the narrower sense of the word. Lexicology, the discipline dealing with dictionaries, must, however, not restrict itself to this sort of study. A dictionary is not merely an accumulation of a large number of individual words; it is a complicated system of items where all words are at once related and mutually exclusive.

The meaning of a word is determined by its relationship within an identical lexicon, i.e. by its place in the particular lexical system. The determination of the place which a particular word occupies in the lexical system is possible only when we determine the structure of this system. Special attention should be paid to such a study because until now hardly any research has been done on words as members of lexical systems, nor has any attempt been made to uncover the structures of these systems. Many linguists have considered the lexicon—as opposed to morphology, which forms a system by definition—as chaos only capable of external organization through arrangement of vocabulary items in alphabetical order. This is obviously erroneous. Of course, lexical systems are so much more complex and comprehensive than morphological systems, and linguists will perhaps never succeed in organizing them with such clarity and explicitness as can be done with morphological systems. Although individual words in the lexicon are both related and mutually exclusive, they nevertheless form systems, and linguistics must study them. Linguists are expected to deal not only with the material itself, but also to work out correct research methods in this as yet almost virgin territory.

Every language has its specific lexical systems at any one time. The individuality of each system stands out clearly, especially in comparison with other such systems; comparing closely related registers is particularly interesting because individual features in the structure of a particular lexical system then stand out with a distinctive clarity. To this end, the Slavic languages provide an unusually suitable and rewarding field of research.

9. *The significance of functional linguistics for Slavic language cultivation and criticism.*

Language cultivation is an effort to reinforce, both in the standard and in the colloquial literary idiom, those features which the special function of literary language requires.

The primary concern is one of *stability*, i.e. of ridding the language of all unnecessary vaccilation and of creating a feeling of linguistic security for the literary language as well; a further concern is *accuracy*, i.e. the ability to render various shades of content clearly and precisely, delicately and effortlessly; finally, there is the individuality of the language, i.e. reinforcement of features characteristic of the language in question. A frequent concern is the choice of one of several alternatives formed in the language in order to transform a latent tendency into an intentionally utilized means of expression.

As far as pronunciation is concerned, the necessity of stabilization follows from the stated principal requirements even in cases where variants have not yet been admitted (e.g. in literary Czech, the cluster spelled *sh* can be pronounced both as /sx/ and /zh/, e.g.

in *shoda* 'agreement'; or the question of the pronunciation of *ije*, *je* or *e* in literary Serbo-Croation).

Orthography, as merely a conventional and practical matter, ought to be as easy and synoptic as its function of visual differentiation permits. The frequent alternation of orthographic rules, especially in cases where simplification is not the goal, contradicts the requirement of stability. Discrepancies between the spelling of the native and foreign vocabulary must be eliminated, at least in places where they cause confusion in pronunciation (e.g. in the Czech lexicon, *s* of foreign origin has the value of both /s/ and /z/).

The individuality of language ought to be kept in mind when dealing with forms of denotation; that is, forms foreign to the target language (e.g. compounds in Czech) should not be used unless this is absolutely unavoidable. As for the lexicon, the principle of a rich, stylistically varied vocabulary should be measured against the requirement of lexical purism. Accuracy and stability should be respected as much as versatility when the function of the literary language requires it.

Syntax should be scrutinized both in terms of the individual expressive power of the language and in the richness of expressive means differentiated in their meaning. It is then necessary to enforce features idiosyncratic to the language in question (e.g. a tendency toward verbal expression in Czech). Syntactic purism, however, must not narrow the inventory of expressive means whose justification— even in syntax, has to be determined by the function of language (as in the need for nominal constructions in legal or other professional language).

The importance of morphology for the individual expressive power of language rests in its general system, not in peculiarities of detail. Therefore, from the functional standpoint it does not have the importance ascribed to it by purists of the old type. The gap between the written and the colloquial language should not be widened by unnecessary morphological archaisms.

The cultivated colloquial idiom is very important for culture; it serves as a constant and safe source of revival for the written language. It creates an environment in which it is safe to cultivate the language feeling necessary for the stability of the written language.

Both the colloquial and the spoken literary language constitute expressive means of cultural life which in each nation takes much from the common cultural fund of the entire pertinent educated stratum; therefore the cultural community is naturally reflected in the literary language, and it would be incorrect to fight this phenomenon in the name of language purity.

It follows from the above comment that patronage of language purity has its place in language cultivation. Every exaggerated form of purism, however, be it based on logic, historicity, or folklore, impairs the true cultivation of literary language.

Concern for language cultivation is imperative for the majority of Slavic literary languages due to their relatively youthful tradition or an interrupted or hasty development.

Intensive work in the areas of formation of Slavic literary languages has been undertaken recently, even in groups which lack an established literary tradition. Applied linguistics has an important role in this area: the selection from among phonological and grammatical variants of those variants which are most advantageous for the literary language, be it either for their values of differentiation or their capacity for expansion; the design of a script and an orthography which is not guided by a striving for phonetic transcription and considerations of a diachronic nature, but rather which would be determined by synchronic phonology where a maximum degree of graphic economy would be achieved while expressing phonological correlations; the creation of a dictionary, especially one for terminology. Nationalistic or archaic puristic considerations should not interfere here, because exaggerated purism impoverishes the lexicon; brings about a surplus of synonyms and undue etymological links between items of terminology and words in daily use, an association and an emotional coloring harmful for terminology; and, finally, an excessive local conservativism in scientific terminology.

10. *The application of the new linguistic trends in secondary*

school.

a. Application in instruction in the mother tongue.

1. Historical comparative linguistics has contributed very little to the solution of the practical problems of how to teach the mother tongue in high schools; the object of such research was merely the development of language with primary emphasis on older periods of evolution. As far as contemporary language is concerned, closer attention must be paid to dialect than to literary language.

New trends in linguistics can provide a safer basis for the solution of practical problems; common points between modern linguistics and the task of mother tongue instruction in secondary schools are as follows:

Synchronic language features are the subject of synchronic linguistics, i.e. always language of one period, primarily the contemporary period: this subject brings synchronic linguistics closer to its role in high school because contemporary literary language has once more become the subject of linguistic research.

Functional linguistics views language as a sum of expedient means which are defined by various functions of the language. The ability to utilize language means economically and rationally in accord with purpose and situation, i.e. developing the capacity to comply best with the specific function of language on specific occasions as, for example, in a dialogue, in all kinds of documents, in reflection, etc.—this constitutes the goal of native language instruction in secondary schools.

The concept of language as a functional system and an effort to define the exact characteristics of the individual contemporary languages can provide a more secure basis for the classification of language phenomena and for their interpretation even in secondary schools.

2. The basic difference between scientific linguistic research and the role of the secondary school with respect to the mother tongue is naturally the fact that the goal of school instruction is the best possible practical mastery of the language in its various fucntions associated with cultural life, above all a mastery of the standard literary language. The difference between instruction in

linguistic science and the mother tongue is equally significant: the acquisition of a certain amount of linguistic knowledge is not the role of mother tongue instruction.

Equally important is the difference between foreign language instruction and the teaching, or better, cultivation, of the mother tongue: concern for the mother tongue is a gradual development of language awareness which the students bring with them and which in certain situations is quite precise and elaborate.

3. The scholastic (theoretical) goal of mother tongue instruction retreats behind this practical (technical) aim, and the extent of theoretical instruction for language practice in special functions of literary language (see Article 8) can be determined appropriately for each grade and kind of school from the general educational and cultural point of view.

4. A knowledge of the facts of historical phonology, morphology, dialect classification, etc. contributes little to the gradual language development mentioned above. The consideration of language as a whole, where the student distinguishes between language means known and unknown to him up to that point, where he recognizes the ways in which they can be utilized and considers how a goal has been reached by employing them, contributes very effectively to gradual language development. Also extremely productive are the students' own experiments where they attempt to satisfy a specific functional task by utilization of known language means. This functional task naturally begins with the simplest communicative function and only gradually becomes more complicated. In this way, vocabulary, denominative, and relational means (or, in traditional terminology, lexicon, morphology, semantics, and syntax in a narrower or broader sense) are being developed and refined and the means of their application recognized. Such an approach should not be limited only to written manifestations of language. Spoken utterances and their phonic aspects should also be considered and cultivated.

5. From the function of standard literary language, it follows that its cultivation cannot be completed before the student has gained insight into the content aspect of areas intrinsic to the liter-

ary language; on the contrary, refinement of the literary language in areas where it differs from the folk idiom is the task of the higher secondary school grades.

6. The students must recognize that literary language differs according to the purpose of its usage, that the basis of a correct and expressive style lies in its adequacy for the purpose and that the evaluative hierarchy of styles from simple to decorative has to be completely eliminated.

7. From the outset, it is necessary (for practical reasons) to emphasize gradually those aspects where the phonological and grammatical system of the literary language differs from the common popular idiom known to students from their families and daily life. It is absolutely unnecessary, however, to emphasize aspects common to both. Quite the contrary, close attention should be paid that the student develop the confidence in his own knowledge of his mother tongue and build on this knowledge.

8. The acquired information about language should be conceptualized in an understanding of the language systems; language study and the unveiling of its system have a different significance for the student than does general language instruction. Awareness of the system is important for language practice, whose concern is the conscious and expedient expression and production necessary in the functions of literary language.

b. On Slavic language teaching.

1. It has been generally recognized that the acquisition of a foreign Slavic language in school must be of a practical nature. Such acquisition used to be quite distinct from scientific interpretation in which only a historical-comparative study was recognized as valid. A separation of scientific historical-comparative study from practical knowledge is, from the standpoint of contemporary linguistics, prejudicial. Even practical language acquisition ought to be scientifically based and justified.

Historical-comparative linguistics cannot provide the scientific basis for practical language acquisition. Practical language instruction requires an understanding of the language in, above all, its particular function, in a particular social environment, and under specific conditions, for language research which disregards the concrete functions of language is a mere abstraction. This is one reason why functional linguistics, which views language as a system or means employed by a speaker or group of speakers in accordance with the purpose of the utterance, provides the possibility of solving this problem scientifically.

2. It is generally known that there are few people who can master all functions of their mother tongue equally well. It often happens that even a philologically educated individual is able to produce an application, an announcement or a news report only with difficulty or even not at all if the subject is not in his field. This fact offers guidelines for practical language instruction: e.g. in commercial schools to acquire a mastery of language used for commercial purposes (colloquial business idiom, correspondence and journalistic idiom, the idiom of technical business reports, etc.); in secondary schools in the narrower sense, in contrast to professional schools, the concern is the students' mastery of the general, cultivated idiom (i.e. the language of the educated class without any special professional coloring, both in written and spoken form).In addition to special functions, it is always necessary to recognize and master language facts that have elementary social purposes such as greetings, introductory phrases, and questions about the weather, time, etc., but such elements are relatively few; all language instruction can start with these items.

3. The utilization of the relation between Slavic languages is necessary for their instruction in Slavic schools. This ought to be done in such a way that not only common elements will be explained and their application practiced from the beginning of instruction (lectures) and in textbooks, but above all those aspects where a language system of one Slavic language differs from that of another are to be stressed. Both instruction and textbooks have to be differential, grounded in the diversity between the students' mother tongue and the target language.

4. The idiosyncratic features of the phonological system should be considered both in their realization in pronunciation and in their manifestation in orthography. The characteristic features of

the grammatical system of a particular Slavic language should also be observed. Their acquisition proceeds gradually via context, not individual words. The details of the process are determined by the particular Slavic language, by the Slavic environment where this language is studied, and by the type and level of school, as well as by the general level of the students' education. For example, when describing the Russian phonological system to Czechs, we emphasize the alternation of hard and soft consonants, the reduction of unstressed vowels, the primary role of accent; in a characterization of the Czech phonological system for Russians, we stress the role of quantity, its independence of stress, the grammatical alternation of prepalatal and postpalatal vowels under certain conditions (a consequence of so-called "umlaut"), etc. The delineation of lexical forms must emphasize productive inflectional forms, the description of group forms (so-called "syntax"), and important differences (for Russian these are: the role of modals, the expression of necessity and possibility, complex verbal expressions, prepositions, conjunctions and their function, etc.).

As far as the lexicon is concerned, we believe it proper that its acquisition be based on context and on individual information, so that the overall process has the form of the students' decoding of the target language, and not the nature of mere instruction in the language as decoded by the teacher, as is common in the case of unrelated or dead languages (Latin, Greek, etc.). In this way, comprehension would prevail over mere recognition. Naturally, even the recognition of the lexicon of each individual Slavic language has important peculiarities, e.g. for Russian it is very important to show the layer of Church Slavic elements and their stylistic significance (*glava* 'chapter, summit, leader' : *golova* 'head'; *otvratit* 'to avert' : *otvorotit* 'to turn aside'; *isčerpat* 'exhaust (argument)', etc. : *vyčerpat* 'exhaust, scoop out, bail out', etc.

5. One should avoid asserting greater agreement than actually exists between one's own language and the target language; it happens that the functions of categories of another Slavic language are superimposed on the mother tongue system; a characteristic Pan-Slavic language thus originates— Czecho-Russian, Serbo-Polish,

Russo-Bulgarian, etc. The functions of categories have to be examined primarily within their own language system.

6. It follows from the above analysis that, in accordance with the given guidelines, the most important methodological-didactic problem is to produce textbooks, chrestomathies, and aids which would facilitate mastery of the target language in its specific functions. A set of such aids would provide a secure basis for language acquisition which the student could develop as required by concrete circumstances and by the social environment which he enters.

NOTES

1. Originally published as congress material under the title: *I. Sjezd slovanských filologů v Praze 1929. Sekce II. These k diskusi. 1er congrès des philologues slaves à Prague 1929. Section IIème. Propositions 1-9.* [The First Congress of Slavic Philologists in Prague, 1929. Section II. Theses for Discussion]. Part 10 was published in the theses of *Sekce III* [Section III] as *These k diskusi* [Theses for Discussion] — *Section IIIème, Propositions 2a, 2b.*

BY WAY OF INTRODUCTION[1]

What can a discipline dealing with language, namely linguistics, offer a standard literary language? Must it stop with proclamations of conservative laws and prohibitions, or is it capable of making positive contributions to the development of the language? The response depends upon what kind of linguistics we have in mind.

The time when the quest for origin was of greater interest than the neglected problems of purpose and intent is not long past. Linguistics in the second half of the last century presents a conspicuous example of this attitude. Every linguistic fact was interesting primarily as a variant of a certain older fact, and for that reason emphasis was placed on the problem of what was substituted for what and why this happened. The question "why" was answered by explaining the physiological conditions of the change and the mechanics of individual psychological associations. When we hear or read a speech utterance, the question of its sense and purpose presents itself quite naturally, but the linguistics of the recent past completely eliminated this problem. The famous Russian linguist Fortunatov was embarrassed when asked about the content of the manuscripts whose language he had just finished analyzing. Language is a totality only when viewed from the angle of purpose. A complete atomization was the immediate consequence when investigation of the tasks and aims of language was excluded from linguistics, which, instead of being a science dealing with language in its totality, has become a collection of data on scattered language facts.

Disagreement with this point of view emerged, particularly at the hands of the Geneva linguist Ferdinand de Saussure, who well understood that a scientific analysis of language must not be restricted to historical problems. Saussure attempted a statistical cross-section of language and overcame the common mechanistic point of view in the problems of language statistics by viewing language as a system of objective values. In this, Saussure became one of the modern pioneers of linguistic research. As far as questions of language development are concerned, however, Saussure followed in the footsteps of traditional mechanistic views and directly proclaimed linguistic changes to be blind and incidental and mankind incapable of changing anything in language; linguistics was confined to language as it is. Saussure's Prague contemporary and a student of Brentano,[2] Anton Marty,[3] advanced much further in this question as he applied the problem of intent not only to language statistics but also to language evolution. Toward his unjustifiable generalization of the thesis of a lack of planning in language development, however, Marty made only partial progress. For him, language is a "planlose Absicht"; initiators of language innovations are aware of neither the language as a totality nor of the functions of its parts, nor of the final effect of an innovation on the totality, nor of the methodological principles of the changes which they themselves have carried out. The innovators keep in mind only the subject, only the communicative goals, while language values remain in the shadows because the linguists' attention is not focused on language as such. Marty presents the relation between language sign and its purpose relatively correctly, but his findings require considerable limitation. As early as 1887, another follower of Brentano, T. G. Masaryk,[4] stated precisely that for us speakers language is not an independent object, but only a representative of the world of objects, only a means of information about them. He adds, however, that in spite of this, linguistics makes language an object of scientific research as an end in itself.

This reflection can be continued further. Not only science converts language from a mere means to an end; language politics, language pedagogy, and language criticism also do so. It is correct to say that conjunctions cannot function as subjects in a sentence, but when we reflect on them, we may say for example " 'and' is a conjunction," and, in that sentence, the conjunction "and" becomes a subject. Our relation to a language sign is similarly changed as soon as this sign becomes an independent object of our reflections— be it in linguistics, language politics, or pedagogy. An identical shift can be observed in language criticism. Even there, language functions as a substance, "as a separate work next to the material world and the world of thought," in Masaryk's words.[5]

The basic function of poetry, no matter how it is viewed, shows without doubt that poetry provides the language sign with a certain autonomy. Rhyme, for example, represents a confrontation of two harmonious words. This confrontation is unnecessary for communicative purposes, but it reveals language values and bestows partial independence upon them: the harmony of rhymed words draws attention to their vocal composition, and whether we wish it or not, we also pay attention to the phenomena of possible grammatical identity and relationship in meaning. In sum, in our contact with language there exists a whole series of situations where language becomes a direct object of our attention. In these situations, the concern is not only our relation to the object of the verbal manifestation, but also directly to the manifestation in and of itself. This relation becomes an immediate component of the language structure. This transformation of language from means, from a mere representative of the objective world into an independent object of our attention, our reflections, our emotions— this relation to language can be defined as language cultivation.

****

Language cultivation manifests itself in varied socio-historical situations. For example, if a peasant wants to use an urban idiom and he learns and intentionally imitates it, it is a phenomenon of language cultivation, more precisely characterized as one of language pedagogy. If, however, this person ridicules another peasant's pronunciation, be it out of local patriotism (everything that is our own is better) or for social reasons (his way of speech represents a symbol of social inferiority to him), both phenomena belong to the domain of language cultivation— more precisely, language criticism. Language itself is the object of attention and ceases to be merely a means of communication, a mere reference to an object. As soon as language becomes an independent object of observation and reflection, then Marty's thesis that language as a whole and the functioning of its parts are beyond the scope of the speaker's attention, loses validity. His conclusion regarding the unplanned execution of language intent also collapses. It is clear that the number of planned components in language evolution increase with the growing demands of language pedagogy, language criticism, and language politics. We know from economics that anarchy of production is not a constantly unchangeable category outside of any time dimension, but only a historical stage. Equally, the question of language of a lower or higher degree of planning in language economy is a question of cultural evolution. Language cultivation flourishes with an expansion of culture in general, and when language cultivation thrives, there is an increase of systematic interventions by society in language development.

The following basic problems of language cultivation require systematic treatment:

1. *Language law*, both in theory and in practice; and

2. *language pedagogy,* i.e. a person's perfection of his mother tongue from childhood through higher education, foreign language instruction, the struggle against pathological phenomena, etc.; and

3. *language construction,* i.e. on the one hand the working out and codification of language norms (orthoepic, orthographic, grammatical, lexical, and phraseological); on the other hand, the determination of pertinent ideological and esthetic demands on the language, and, finally, an application of these demands and norms on concrete language manifestations (language criticism).

All these problems are urgent today, but at the same time they are unusually complicated and intricate. There are several causes of this state of affairs, the following in particular: the language question has a prominent place in the complex of contemporary socio-political questions since new needs arise with the gradual democratization of culture in general, and language cultivation in particular. Contemporary science requires detailed, accurate yet flexible, terminology with an international unity of meaning. Language functions are becoming more and more differentiated. One can see this clearly by considering how many new tasks journalism imposes on language. The profession is constantly developing, its importance is increasing steadily: it is newspaper technology itself, problems of fast and easy reading, how to produce an effect on the reader, etc. With the development of new technical means, language finds itself in new, unusual situations. On the radio, we have words as mere sound abstracted from visual perceptions; in sound film there are never-dreamt-of possibilities for the combination of spoken language and visual impressions. Finally, the language of belles lettres defies a uniform code now more than ever; language criticism must not apply an identical scale for the evaluation of a surrealistic poem with the tendency toward a dream, the literature of Joyce and Vančura,[6] where several levels polyphonically transpire; Céline's[7] or Hašek's[8] rich utilization of the colloquial idiom, or the prose of classical realism, meticulously clinging to the generally valid standard norm of literary language. The tremendously increased translation activity forms a special source of new tasks. One look at the number of translations in the area of belles lettres, in periodicals, and in professional literature is sufficient for us to realize what a great linguistic impact these translations have. At the same time it is precisely this translation activity that yields half-finished products because people with the least language qualifications operate there. This is the reason why, particularly there, supervision by language criticism is urgent, and why precisely this is the most profitable area for language therapy and prophylaxis.

When we talk about language criticism, the area we have in mind is not only formal criticism, which deals with an abstract language sign or, more exactly, with an abstracted system of signs in themselves, but also the type of criticism which asks the question of accuracy and adequacy of the language sign, its suitability in relationship to purpose; that is, a purely thematic, ideological criticism. Let us take a look at the philosophical literature of Husserl's school or the new Russian publishing and translation activity, or at Karel Čapek's brilliant essays about the phrase;[9] in spite of varying points of departure, we observe everywhere an effort for a strict control of language signs. The question whether particular language signs are adequate and sufficiently effective is constantly asked. In short, the relationship between the language sign and the denoted object is constantly controlled. War has been declared on language which unjustifiably conceals or distorts theme, as well as on non-matter-of-fact language which loses its relationship to reality, be it concrete or abstract. A new slogan of language responsibility is being formulated with increasing urgency and deliberation.

Our science must not inactively observe the solution of presently delineated tasks. Even Czech linguistics must permanently overcome its temporary breach with the cultural present and place itself in its service; Czech linguistics must take the initiative in solving the immediate problems of language cultivation. The scattered efforts of individual linguists do not suffice here; the urgency of the tasks call for a collective, organized unity of scientific forces. Isolated activity on the point of linguists is insufficient; their close cooperation with pedagogues and lawyers, with philosophers and psychologists, with psychiatrists and phonoatrists, with historians and theoreticians of literature and art in general, with professionals in sociology, history, geography, and ethnography is indispensable. Primarily, however, cooperation is needed with the practical agents of language cultivation, with writers and translators, with agents for theater, film, and radio, both artistic and technical, with professionals in education and workers in administration and technology, all those who have practical experience with questions concerning terminology.

This is the program and the direction of the journal *Slovo a slovesnost* [Word and Verbal Art]. The Prague Linguistic Circle intends to contribute to the many-sided description, criticism, and regulation of contemporary literary Czech in its diversity of cultural tasks and thus implement the principles formulated in its hitherto published works, especially in the collection *Spisovná čeština a jazyková kultura* [Literary Czech and Language Culture].

Individual language phenomena must not be selected casually, neither in the description, criticism, nor regulation of language. Consequently, consideration has to be given to the fact that language is not an incidental accumulation of diffused fragments, but a totality with regular correlations among its individual elements.

Critical and regulatory work should pay close attention to the mutlifaceted task of literary language and avoid its impoverishment.

We will pay close attnetion to the experiences of other countries, both in the positive and in the negative sense. We are aware that our journal is the first attempt of its kind in our country, because similar journals usually stop with the problems of academic science or deal with only a small fragment of language cultivation problems (questions of historical correctness and language purity, printing needs, etc.).

A subject for consideration in *Slovo a slovesnost* will naturally also be literary Slovak, which is just now going through a period of intense cultural expansion and crisis connected with this expansion. We will deal with phenomena common to both Czech and Slovak and also to the particularities of Slovak language development and its contemporary range of problems. Neither is it possible to avoid the practical language problems of Carpathian Ruthenia[10] which have usually been approached from a one-sided genetic point of view. Finally, the basic language problems of national minorities in Czechoslovakia are also going to be included in the body of subjects with which *Slovo a slovesnost* will deal.

****

An essential part of the program of *Slovo a slovesnost* is the complex of problems concerning poetry. Poetry is connected with our area of interest mainly via language, the material of poetry. Josef Jungmann[11] understood the close connection between poetry and language completely when he used the Russian name "Slovesnost"[12] as the title for his book on the theory of verbal art. He comments on his right to do so in the introduction: "Verbal art includes those arts which use only words as means for carrying out their work, e.g. poetry, in contrast to other arts (music, painting, architecture, which need sound, color, construction materials for the execution of their work).[13] When we use Jungmann's term in the title of our publication, we are doing so with direct programmatic intent. We want to express our conviction that language analysis without regard to poetry is as incomplete as an analysis of poetry without regard to words. The esthetic function of language is naturally specific and by its specificity it contrasts with the other functions of language (a verbal manifestation as an end in itself is contrasted here with language as a means to an end). The theoretical disclosure of intent, with which the poet uses the language in each case, is necessary not only for the reader's understanding of the poetic work, but also for the development and focus of the poetic technique itself. It must not be forgotten that literary language frequently draws energy for its evolution from poetry and poetic language. Although peculiarities of poetic language do not always become part of the literary norm (at least it does not happen immediately), poetry constantly illuminates the language system. Each time— from a different angle— it teaches us how to utilize old tools in an unusual way, it causes shifts in the hierarchy of language elements, it refurbishes the stock of stylistic framework, etc. Only poetry mediates the experience of the act of speech in its entire vitality and reveals language not as a rigid system but as creative energy.

Our program is not, however, limited merely to the linguistic material of poetry, but concentrates on poetry as a whole, even on the entire world of art. Poetic work forms a structure, i.e. a unity, where the individual components become explicit only in connection with all other components, a practically insoluble unity and yet dynamic in the sense that its components do not function as dead building material, but constitute reciprocally operative, at times contrastive, forces. This is why it is impossible to deal with a work of poetry while ignoring its subject, or to analyze the phonic structure of a poem while ignoring its composition, etc.

The relationship between language problems and problems of the other kinds of art is more complex. It is specified by the problem of the sign, which is one of the most urgent philolosophical problems in the cultural rebirth of our time. All reality, from sensory perception to the most abstract mental construct, appears to modern man as a vast, intricately organized realm of signs. An examination of this realm is only at its beginning, however. Therefore, it is necessary to pay attention to, above all, those spheres of human culture where the varying internal organization of the sign is revealed in its entire complexity. One such sphere is undoubtedly language. Although not the simplest, it is the fundamental system of signs, because the constant tendency to express everything in verbal terms exists in the entire realm of signs. Language can be especially instructive in the area of referential relationship, i.e. the relationship between a sign and the reality to which the sign refers, because both written and spoken language aim, above all, at expressing and acting upon reality, even indirectly. Art, on the other hand, be it poetry or any other kind of art, provides exemplary material for studying the internal structure of the sign itself, for examining the relationship between symbol (e.g. sound, color, etc.) and its meaning, and for the investigation of the manifold stratification of meaning. This is because the objective relationship within art is broken down; a work of art is not evaluated by the truthfulness of its message; it is a sign in itself, hovering freely between the artist and his audience. This special character of art stands out particularly in the study of poetry, which is anchored at an intersection between language and art.

Any study of poetic language and poetry implies, by definition, consideration of society and its organization. Sign, by its essence, is a social phenomenon. It is used for mediation between members of a certain group and understood only on the basis of the entire system of values common to this group. In language, which is proximate to both subjects—the one which furnishes the sign and the one which perceives it—there is a third firm point which stretches the texture of the internal composition of the sign; it is the reality toward which the sign points. As asserted above, this objective relationship is broken down in poetry and art. The dependence of the sign on society is emphasized still more. Although a work of art is a world in itself (or perhaps just because it is), it cannot be perceived and evaluated in any way other than in its relationship to the system of values valid in a specific collective. The connection between art and society is naturally manifold, and all sorts of indirectness and antitheses are possible here. In addition, society does not represent an undifferentiated, homogeneous unit in relationship to art. The enitre dynamics of social development, the regrouping and struggle of individual social strata and settings, as well as class, national, and ideological struggle, all are reflected with intensity in the relationship between art and society and in the evolution of art itself, although changes in artistic structures form a coherent and regular sequence. Questions arise such as whether the social origin of the artists in a specific period is identical with the class for which they are creating, whether art in a specific period responds to the social order of that period or whether it is created in opposition to it, whether a specific type of art is, on the entire scale of its kind, created for one social class, or whether the representatives of different artistic species of one identical art type originate in different social strata, etc. To arouse interest in these problems, to stimulate and organize studies and symposia dealing with the relationship between poetry (especially Czech) and society, is also one of the important tasks of our journal.

Finally, we do not intend to avoid the problem of the personality of the poet, being well are of the antinomy between individual disposition and the active abilities of the poet on the one hand and the objective evolutional conditions, independent of the artist, on the other.

****

Neither do we intend to neglect the questions of the past. The Czech language's past, verbal art, and linguistics are indissolubly linked with the problems of the present, and tradition is always one of the most delicate constituents of any cultural construction. At times, we have been criticized for insufficient respect for the Czech scientific past, more precisely for the heritage from the end of the nineteenth century. Unjustly so. We are all well aware of the great work which this period accomplished for the history of Czech culture, especially by the Gebauer[14] generation, and we understand that one-sided atomistic historicism was a prerequisite for this generation. It would certainly reflect a naive egocentrism to criticize the scholars of the 1890s for not anticipating the problems of the 1930s. It would be equally naive, however, to demand from the science of the latter period that it give up, in the name of the glorious past, solving the scientific problems of its own day. Modern Czechoslovak linguistic research is focused not only on an emphatic formulation of an entire set of problems of the synchronic type, so remote from the preceding generation of scientists, and of the bond between the statics and dynamics of language, but it also has, though this may seem paradoxical at first sight, a broader historical outlook on the Czech linguistic tradition than the historicizing science of the nineties had. At that point, the tradition of linguistic research was limited to what was done in historical linguistics, and older research was greatly overlooked. This is the reason why fruitful Czech attempts of the eighties dealing with the basics of general linguistics and research in the area of the language philosophy of Bolzano,[15] Klácel,[16] Šercl[17] were underestimated, why the magnificent work of language construction done by the Jungmann group was belittled, and why a significant attempt of Tomsa,[18] Dobrovský's[19] contemporary, to create a synchronic Czech grammar remained almost unnoticed. A period deaf to Baroque culture found only words of contempt for the excellent linguist of the Baroque period, Václav Rosa.[20]

The years when the socially and nationally oppressed small-town Czech society struggled hard to gain the basic existential rights of nationhood and the use of its own language could not possibly have a sufficient understanding of the period of big-power expansion in the upper-class culture of the Czech middle ages. Therefore, the two most brilliant periods of Old Czech cultural, particularly linguistic, development have remained neglected. First, there was the period of Cyril and Methodius[21] when a then Czechoslovak state stepped forth as a politically and culturally conscious patron of the first attempt toward a Slavic, indeed Pan-Slavic, literary language; the consequences of this attempt were far-reaching for the cultural history of southern and eastern Slavs. The attempt here collapsed, but the memory of it remained an effective stimulus in the struggle for a national language for church and literature in the Czech Gothic period. We thence arrive at the second period where a grand creativity in language and literature transformed Czech into a literary language of international standing and one well empowered to convey cultural effects. The vocabulary of the Czech language in the Gothic period was, after Church Slavic, the only source which provided almost the entire Slavic world with the terminology of culture. It was none other than literary Czech of the Gothic period that provided an incentive for the inception of literary Polish and enriched the Ukrainian and Russian vocabulary. Some of the Church Slavic elements of the Russian and Czech vocabulary then passed over into the South Slavic languages, particularly into Modern Bulgarian.

For centuries, the Gothic period sustained us, and Ignát Herrmann[22] justifiably contrasts the farsighted, big-power construction of the Prague of Charles IV[23] against the narrow horizons of the Prague of fifty years ago when matters were accomplished only in accordance with latter-day standards. We cannot and will not return to Gothic culture, but the broad-minded, confident, and tenacious construction of that period is a more relevant and a more stimulating model for modern times than the most heroic and sacrificing efforts of the barren yesteryear.

Bohuslav Havránek, Roman Jakobson, Vilém Mathesius, Jan Mukařovský, Bohumil Trnka

NOTES

1. From *Slovo a slovesnost* [Word and Verbal Art], Vol. I (1935), pp. 1-7.
2. Franz Clemens Brentano (1838-1917), an influential professor of philosophy at Würzburg and Vienna; his orientation was empirical, and his observations in the areas of psychology, descriptive and genetic. His major works focused on Aristotle and psychology, e.g. *Zur Klassification der psychischen Phänomene* (1911).
3. Anton Marty(1847-1914), German philosopher and psychologist; taught at the University of Würzburg and at the German University in Prague. Major

works: *Ursprung der Sprache* (1875), *Über das Verhältnis von Grammatik und Logik* (1893), *Über Begriff und Methode der allgemeinen Grammatik und Sprachphilosophie* (1910).

4. Tomáš Garrigue Masaryk (1850-1937), Czech philosopher and statesman; the first president of the Czechoslovak Republic (1918-1937). His ideas as here loosely quoted come from his *Versuch einer concreten Logik* (Vienna: Verlag von Carl Konegen, 1887), pp. 187-194.

5. Ibid.

6. Vladislav Vančura (1891-1942), Czech prose writer distinguished for his masterly use of language. His major (unfinished) work is *Obrazy z dějin národu českého* (1939-40; *Scenes from the History of the Czech People*), written in the style of the old chronicle narrative.

7. Louis Ferdinand Destouches, pseudonym Céline since 1932; French author (1894-1961) who helped destroy the status quo in French literary style by bringing about a breakdown between the written and the spoken idiom.

8. Jaroslav Hašek (1883-1923). In addition to numerous short stories, he is the author of *Osudy dobrého vojáka Švejka za světové války* (1920-23; *The Adventures of the Good. Soldier Švejk During the World War*); distinguished himself by using very colloquial language in his works.

9. Karel Čapek (1890-1938), prolific and versatile Czech writer, translator of French poetry, author of, among other things, the story *Válka s mloky* (1936; *The War with the Newts*), a drama, *Bílá nemoc* (1937; *The White Plague*). Čapek's foresight in his choice of topics (the two works mentioned here deal with the development of fascism and anticipate World War II) and his effective and imaginative use of language place him among the foremost writers of worldwide importance. His preoccupation with words and their meanings is demonstrated in, for example, the collection of essays entitled *V zajetí slov* (1920; enlarged edition 1969, *Captive of Words*).

10. *Subcarpathian Ruthenia*: Eastern part of Czechoslovakia between World Wars I and II. Now part of the Ukrainian Republic of the Soviet Union.

11. Josef Jungmann (1773-1847), a student of Dobrovský (see fn. 19); propagated usage of the Czech language in all fields of national scholarship; strove for the development of poetry in the classical spirit. Major works: *Slowesnost* (1820; *Verbal Art* [see fn. 12]), *Historie literatury české* (1825; *History of Czech Literature*); *Slovník česko-německý* (1835-39; *Czech-German Dictionary*).

12. *Slovesnost* translates literally as "verbal art." Jungmann's work has not been translated into English. In his translation of Arne Novák's *Czech Literature* (Ann Arbor: Michigan Slavic Publications, 1976), Peter Kussi (p. 132) gives the title of Jungmann's work as "Literature," which, though correct, covers but one aspect of the word *slovesnost*. The complete title of Jung-

mann's work is as follows: *Slowesnost, aneb zbjrka přikladů s krátkým poged-nánjm o slohu* [Verbal Art, Or a Collection of Examples with a Short Treatise on Style].

13. Josef Jungmann, *Slowesnost* (Prague, 1820), p. VIII. The original citation is as follows: "Básnjctwj a řečnjctwj od hudebnjctvj tjm se dělj, že toto city prostředkem pauhých zwuků, onano prostředkem wýražných, srozumitedlných hlasů, t. slow wygadřuje, odkudž uměnj slowesná anebo slowesnost krátce nazwána býti mohau." [The distinction between poetry and rhetoric on the one hand and music on the other lies in the fact that the former two use expressive, intelligible voices; that is, words, while the latter uses merely sounds. Therefore the former two can be called, in brief, verbal arts.]

14. Jan Gebauer (1838-1907), an outstanding Czech Bohemicist; author of the monumental *Historická mluvnice jazyka českého* (1894; *An Historical Grammar of the Czech Language*) and *Slovník staročesky* (1901-07; *A Dictionary of Old Czech*); editor of *Listy filologické* (*Philological Journal*) since 1874.

15. Bernard Bolzano (1781-1848), Czech philosopher and mathematician, from 1805 professor at the University of Prague; Prague leader of the Catholic Enlightenment which sought to reconcile theological teaching with new philosophic and scientific findings by emphasizing tolerant Christianity. He was expelled from the university by the Jesuits in 1820. Among his works: *Wissenschaftslehre* (1837), *Erbauungsreden für Akademiker* (1849-51).

16. František Matouš Klácel (1808-1882), a Catholic lyricist; author of celebratory and didactic poetry; persecuted for his adherence to Hegelian philosophy and to pantheism; emigrated to America (August, 1869), where he died. Major linguistic work: *Počátky vědeckého mluvnictví českého* (1843; *The Beginnings of Scientific Czech Grammar*).

17. Čeněk Šercl (1843-1906), originally a lawyer. His profound interest in language led to extensive travel (England, Finland, Russia) and to prolific linguistic productivity. He eventually became a professor in Kharkov and Odessa. Among his most important works, written in Russian: *Sanskritskaja grammatika* (1873; *Sanskrit Grammar*), *O konkretnosti v jazykach* (1885; *On the Concrete in Language*).

18. František Jan Tomsa (1753-1814), one of the major representatives of the Czech National Revival. In addition to minor prose works in the areas of belles lettres and religion, he also wrote linguistic works: *Böhmische Sprachlehre* (1782), *Ueber die Aussprache der čechischen Buchstaben Sylben und Wörter* (1800), *Ueber die čechische Rechtschreibung* (1802).

19. Josef Dobrovský (1753-1829), Czech priest, supporter of the reforms of Emperor Josef II; the most significant scholar of the Czech National Revival; applied strict rational criticism is his search for scientific truth based on facts. His areas of interest cover Slavic linguistics, literary history, and critical

historical research. His writings are in Latin and German, and his most important works in the area of linguistics are: *Deutsch-Böhmisches Wörterbuch* (1802-1821), *Aüsfuhrliches Lehrgebäude der böhmischen Sprache* (1819), *Institutiones linguae slavicae dialecti veretis* (1822).

20. Václav Rosa (1620-1689), a lawyer by profession; major linguistic work: *Čechořečnost, seu Grammatica linguae Bohemicae* (1672), a work in four parts— the first three in Latin, the last in Czech.

21. Cyril (827-869) and Methodius (d. 885), brother missionaries; brought liturgical and literary language based on Macedonian-Bulgarian dialect into the Great Moravian Empire. Originally two scripts existed: Glagolitic and Cyrillic; both were derived from the Greek alphabet. The Slavs were given religious literature imbued with Byzantine-Greek ideology. The Old Church Slavic tradition persisted in the East and South Slavic areas to a greater extent than in the Czech area.

22. Ignát Hermann (1854-1935), Czech writer and journalist; masterful in portraying the common "little people" of Prague.

23. Charles IV (1310-1378), Roman emperor and Czech king; his broad-minded politics promoted the Czech lands politically, economically, and culturally to worldwide importance.

TOWARD A SEMANTIC ANALYSIS OF PHILOSOPHICAL TEXTS[1]

Ladislav Rieger

1. Prior to presenting illustrations of semantic analyses, it is useful to clarify the word "semantic" and the methods of analysis. The word is of Greek origin: "sema" in prose, "semeion" in poetry means sign; it is "something that stands for something else." In the broadest sense of the word, we talk about speech as a system of signs because "all speech indicates or means something," as Aristotle commented. In a narrower sense of the word, the concern here is not human language, but the function of the sign, of designation. Other manifestations can also represent something for us, e.g. animal expressions and, indirectly, even natural phenomena (smoke means fire; fever, sickness) or interpretations of manifestations of other beings (in a myth, fairy-tale, folk belief, etc.). Naturally, individual incoherent cries, facial expressions, and gestures (of the deaf-and-dumb and others), all artificial (even traffic) signals, and naturally the so-called "language of the arts" (creative arts, music, verbal art, etc.) also belong within this concept of language. It is obvious that the purpose of all these various functions of language is not merely "to report, to tell about something" (an apophantic function) as Aristotle realized long ago (he gives a prayer as an example). The emotive function is evident in art and has its importance even in philosophy, as we shall see.

2. The discipline dealing with signs is of ancient origin, even though it has attained its full development only in very recent times. Ancient beginnings are not without importance (see, e.g., K. Svoboda in *Časopis pro moderní filologii*, Vol. 26 [1940], p. 4); these attempts were to some extent carried further by the scholastics, but they lack logical refinement and clarity. They are frequently tied to preconceived analogies (e.g. St. Augustine sees the relationship of sign to its meaning as a relationship between body and soul). Mainly, however, these attempts represent a fusion of grammar and logic. Only modern logic is founded on a

purely formal basis, and so-called "semiotics" or "semiology," its logical refinement, dates from modern times and is not yet complete.

Linguistics, naturally, has its own territory— in a sense more advanced and specialized, apart from the circle of logicians. I do not mean merely fundamental works and schemes of language, as e.g. Bühler's *Axiomatik der Sprachwissenschaften* (Kantstudien, Vol. 38, 1932), but primarily the work of the Prague Linguistic Circle. The structural concept of language as a system of signs represents progress in comparison with Bühler's concept of isolated sign. The system as a whole gives meaning to its components in accordance with their place in the development and with regard to the tension between the existing language and the actual needs of expression. An analysis of meaning has then not only a static, but also a dynamic aspect, and a system of signs does not represent merely a total set with fixed meaning which is simply at one's disposal. At the same time, it is a living reality subject to recurrent modernization. These relationships are naturally very complex; actually, they reflect the entire cultural history of mankind. Thus, it will not be without interest to call attention to the abstractly analytical method which logic uses for language analysis. Even when the results at times appear too primitive for advanced linguistics, the method itself allows for work even on special tasks and provides a clear and definite survey of the basic facts. The overall view applies more consistently even in logic; compared to the rigor of a purely formal analysis of sign language appropriate in physical sciences (logical syntax à la Carnap), semiotics has been substantially enriched, as we shall see, in the work of Charles Morris,[2] even if his is an analysis of language for the needs of science.

3. Morris uses the following terminology in the study of the basics of the theory of the sign. "Semiotics" to him is a discipline dealing with signs. "Semiosis" is the process in which something functions as a sign. This process involves four factors: 1. *sign* (sign vehicle), the bearer of the sign; 2. *the sign itself* (signum); 3. *the designated object* (designatum); and, finally, 4. *the user of the sign*, be the sign used as a manifestation or as an interpretation. It

is now possible to abstract 1) the purely formal relations of the
sign vehicles among themselves (separated both from their meaning and from the user)— this is the *logical syntax* of language; 2)
the relations of the signs to what they designate (disregarding the
acts of their use)— that is *semantics*, and 3) the relations of the
signs to the users (primarily psychic relations)— this is the *pragmatic dimension of semiotics*. These, then, are the three dimensions or levels of "semiotics."

4. *The syntactic dimension* or level is obtained by an abstraction, not only from the behavior of the user, but also from the
meaning which we subconsciously associate with the sign; that is,
from a semantic relation (signum — designatum). There remain the
purely formal relations among signs arranged in sentences, viz.
possibly the initial position and the permitted alternations or operations, provided that a sentence logically remains a sentence. It
is similar to calculation with algebraic sign vehicles of unknown
value. In this way, it is possible to establish rules of syntax; that is,
the laws of arrangement and rearrangements of the sign vehicles. It
is evident that the so-called "validity" or "correctness" of mathematical (and logical) operations and propositions does not depend
on their user or on their being used at all, or even on a specific
meaning ascribed to them by someone. For example, the validity
of the Pythagorean theorem does not depend at all on its historical
origin, or on the frequency, or even correctness of its use. Its validity not only does not depend on someone's comprehension or interpretation of the theorem, but also not even on whether anything
is meant by it at all. It is not necessary to be concerned with geometric meaning in calculations with algebraic symbols ($a^2 + b^2 +
c^2$), e.g. "the sum of the squares of the sides is equal to the square
of the hypotenuse in the Euclidian system." One does not have to
be concerned with whole numbers which correspond to the equa-
tion. The theorem is simply a point of departure and certain operations are allowed beyond its application. A game of chess has a
certain initial position and certain operations are permissible without even having chessmen and the chessboard, or without considering the genesis of the meaning of the chess game (king, etc.);

letters and numbers suffice, that is to say signs, and we are dealing with a game of signs. Syntax is nothing but an aggregate of rules of such a game; these rules can be revealed with greatest ease if the entire problem can be simplified by abstracting from all semantic components and from the usage of signs. As we know, only in this way has mathematics achieved exactitude. Logic follows the same path. A mathematical game of a scheme of signs can be interpreted, used for dealing with physical reality. Logical syntax can be utilized in the same way; an explanation of this fact would lead us far afield into the problems of epistemology. Stating this fact suffices here. Through a logical analysis of a language, then, we simply find certain basic forms and certain rules of pure syntax which are formally valid in language in general. Second, there are rules of a particular language, the so-called *descriptive syntax*.

5. Naturally, this logical syntax is the ultimate abstraction; hence the ultimate impoverishment of the language, and therefore it cannot satisfy us in and of itself. It is as if it were a frame of formal possibilities, which naturally cannot be used without the semantic and pragmatic dimension. We neither want to nor can remove these levels permanently from language; we can only temporarily abstract from them for certain purposes of a better perspective and simplification in analysis. But when we talk about syntax, these strata function by themselves: indeed, it is *we* who talk about syntax and mean something by it or abstract something from it; it is not syntax itself. Syntactic analysis in itself is of relatively minor significance for our analysis of philosophical texts, and so we refer to it only in passing. Likewise, the pragmatic analysis (of situation) in and of itself will be put aside here; though, as we said, it is very important for proper interpretation. We will merely point out how "semantic" analysis is in constant contact with pragmatic analysis and how the former inevitably leads to the latter. Philosophical texts result from a continuous tension between the situation of a philosophical process and the system of language, which is directly or indirectly (paradox, antinomy) reflected in a text. But this analysis of the philosophical process in and of itself is a major task that, even in an outline, encom-

passes more than our current problem and the dimensions of this article. The subject of our investigation is, as the title specifies, a "semantic" analysis; therefore, other elements or strata have to remain unilluminated in the background, even though they may form a functional unity. It becomes evident in the analysis of philosophical texts that their proper meaning cannot be divorced from the situation; therefore, that a "semantic" analysis is inadequate because the designatum is not some ready-made object, but an object implemented for us only in the activity of the subject, at least as far as its meaning is concerned. This is true in all cases where we are not dealing merely with a simple factual description but with an appeal to someone else who must implement something from the original situation. Therefore, the sense of philosophical texts is not directly "apophantic," or it is so only conditionally. To the interpreter, the text ought to give an impulse toward such an internal situation where an analogical designation can be used. In this rests the sense of philosophical communication.

The word "sense" is used here instead of purpose, goal, intention; that is, in a teleological sense. Otherwise, this word will not be used in relation to an analysis of sense (= meaning) due to its polysemy: sense = aim, sense of a map = semantic relationship, sense of a sentence = its consequence (it follows from the sentence ...), sense = opinion, but also value and norm. For us, a general, structural unit for semiotic analysis is "meaning."

6. Logic studies semantic relations proper (signum—designatum); mainly because of individual signs and at the same time separately from pragmatic elements. In so doing, it relinquishes the dynamics of semantic tension and obtains certain rules for the simplest, or simplified cases. Naturally, the subject of study in linguistics is far more complex. The reason for the complexity is the fact that logic focuses on the language of "exact sciences." Here, it is not necessary to be concerned either with evolution or with pragmatic relations, as we demonstrated in the case of the Pythagorean theorem. Semantic interpretation is purely objective, intersubjective, equal for everyone. Logic has primarily perfected syntax, even here with regard to applicability, i.e. to purely operational seman-

tics. Consequently, semantics is refined only with regard to its use, and this is even truer about pragmatics— at least in works available to us at present. Pragmatic relations are investigated only as "behavior"; that is, only behavioristically. The above mentioned work of Charles Morris should be accepted with its limitations; nevertheless, his formal explanations of certain fundamental concepts should not be underestimated. Especially where questions of syntax of language (I) or of language (II) are concerned, it is beneficial to know the formal possibilities; i.e. primarily the syntax of the language in which a second language (subject of analysis) is treated. Signs help us survey even the most complicated relations, and the methods of abstract symbolics are not bound to be merely in the service of so-called "physicalism" (of the Viennese school).

7. Language, as we have pointed out, does not serve only as an objective communication of a statement of what is. Even so, such communication is one of its most important functions. Semantic analysis of this function yields approximately the following results: signum always has a designatum, but it does not always refer to something that "is not" in the usual sense or is not here and now; e.g. "nothing," zero, $-$, $\sqrt{}$ -1, a winged horse, a square circle, etc. Of course, when we talk about signs (language II, formal), the signs themselves are "denotata" in the sense of physical objects. It is not always easy to distinguish the twofold object talked about, as in "the Moldau flows through Prague" and "the Moldau has six letters." Furthermore, in objective language, signs are used either generally (universally) as in "something," "thing" . . . or they characterize various objects (e.g. "table"), or, finally, they can refer to a specific thing ("this table here"). Various semantic functions are incorporated in this: the deictic function (index of a certain thing), which can be carried out even by a gesture, a (road) sign, an arrow, and further a characterizing function. The signum, which characterizes a thing, can be its image (a photograph, map, model) or only a symbol. An image has a certain common structure with the thing it depicts, whereas a symbol is more abstract (script, numbers, but also a flag, etc.). Hieroglyphs, for example, lie between symbol and image. The difference between image,

symbol, and index lies in the semantic function. The concept, from the standpoint of semantics, is a rule which determines the use of signs that characterize objects either generally or specifically or uniquely.

8. The problem of how we arrive at unambiguous understanding in ordinary speech leads us from semantics to "pragmatics." How do we know, or how can we make sure that we mean the same thing, e.g. "this cup here"? On the one hand, we can point to the thing (semantic indexical relationship) or more precisely, characterize the thing, especially in time and space with reference to a possible perception; that is, to certain behavior, to actions attached to the intersubjective perceptual components. Thus, in principle, we come to an understanding whether "this cup" is or is not here (whether the waiter took it away, etc.) even though each of us individually sees the situation in another way, in another perspective, in a different light, in a different emotional mood. Then we agree (except in the case of illusions and hallucinations) on the existence of the mentioned object, and consequently, on the unambiguous relationship of the signum to the denotatum. Agreement here is naturally limited to a certain temporal-spatial "stratum" of the object to a certain intersubjective aspect "of the same thing." In everyday life there is nothing more at stake, and when there is, we frequently face misunderstandings and conflicts. To be precise, we cannot talk about identical experiencing of various objects, but only about an identity of a certain semantic, temporal-spatial relationship of the sign as a physical object to another physical object, e.g. of a phoneme to a thing.

9. As mentioned above, greater difficulties occur where the relationship is not only a spatial-temporal one, but where the object exists only in time, e.g. a musical melody; the greatest difficulties are where the relationship is not recordable by the senses (feelings, moods, emotions, changes of mind, etc.). Here, context reflecting the entire situation of the subject in question is frequently helpful when we know analogies to it. This is the reason why in texts which do not deal with simple spatial, objective semantic relationships, considerable space is devoted to a description of the situa-

tion, or to evoking a similar emotional state in the reader. This is a well-known fact from psychological novels, etc. Even though only general relationships and concepts of language are at our disposal, these may be semantically restricted by the context. Strictly speaking, however, the purely personal, particular, and unique in the experience is never transferable. This is true even for such a simple experience as the perception of color: even when another person describes for me in detail "that beautiful shade of red there right now," it is never possible to know whether I experience the same thing; at least it cannot be controlled.

10. The non-communicable occurs under ordinary circumstances; the phenomenon has greater significance in unique or so-called "boundary" situations which frequently occur in philosophy. These are states of consciousness that are abstract and representative (non-personal). Scientific, objective knowledge is a case in point. Furthermore, there are states of consciousness that represent a special turning point, a new form of subjectivity, a new historical stage of philosophical knowledge. These situations provide possibilities for various partially new methods; and, to a certain extent, they can be typologically characterized. But an experienced situation always contains something unique, historically postulated, and, despite all possible analogies, non-repeatable, especially in marginal or exceptional situations. Philosophy, as much as it takes advantage of such situations or prepares for them or leads to them, shares this uniqueness (e.g. the death of Socrates, cf. the conclusion of this article). Interpretation must proceed from that situation to the extent that we are able, via empathy, sympathy, or intuition to grasp it in analogy. The context which ought to make this possible for us is then, in theory, vitually everything that can have or had a relationship in the particular period (or even after it) to the situation in which the particular text was written. In spite of that, if there is no possibility of an analogous situation, it is impossible to illuminate what was originally meant. Situation here is a whole complex of external and internal conditions of life. Thus, it would probably be difficult to come to terms with a person coming from a different civilizational stratum,

e.g. "medieval," in the sense of a text dealing with— even indirectly— the conditions of modern transportation, even if it were possible to demonstrate these for him. Perhaps he would regard it all as the work of the devil, and not even comprehend our internal situation if he did not have a certain phantasy of this type (i.e. a certain world view). If we were able, however, to evoke his understanding— that is empathy or intuition for our view, it would in fact amount to a revolution, a transformation of his internal situation and attitude toward the world, and the man would be, at least in purpose, "modern" as for example Bacon in *New Atlantis*, his most Verneian novel. Only then would we be able to comprehend many modern texts, where all this is simply presumed as a background. Conversely, we must often attain in ourselves such an internal transformation if we wish to penetrate older philosophical and other texts. In the entire history of philosophy, even in its most recent phase, far greater displacements are required than those which through the most diverse changes of historical concepts nevertheless remain rooted in common perceptual reality. Here the ground must be abandoned and there is frequently a transposition into the unknown— which everyone undertakes at his own risk. As these situations are frequently new, or less common, philosophy is not as simply communicable or even learnable as the objective sciences are. Philosophical texts are not, in a literal sense, descriptions of existing objects, but cryptic instructions for activity of thought, appeals to realizations of analogical situations, in which the idea of a particular thinker would be valid and in which a transformation of our particular outlook or attitude would (by intuition) become obvious under the impulse of the text.

11. Let us look at some examples and see that, for the reasons just mentioned, a syntactic-semantic analysis is insufficient— without regard to the situation— to acquire an unambiguous interpretation of philosophical texts. Even in the broadest context, a variety of interpretations are possible, as is evident from a concurrent or subsequent emergence of a number of philosophical schools based on "identical doctrine." For that reason, "outmoded" theories are

also revived in new interpretations, or in the light of a new situation, and these interpretations again help create new situations.
Language is far more capable of giving a true picture of the common situations in practical daily life than adequately demonstrating changed situations or even providing directions to a train of
thought required for a change in view for the creation of a new
situation. For example, it is difficult to comprehend abstractly
and describe, let alone implement, the situation of mythical consciousness in concrete terms where I, the thing and the image,
merge or transpire (as in a dream), where the semantic function
proper ceases, since there is not distance or difference between
them. The one "is" the other, it does not "represent" the other.
That is almost the "lower limit" of verbal communication. An
"upper limit" exists as well in areas where consciousness transcends existentially, not potentially, but actually, into being; even
here, only silence remains (see the conclusion of this article).
Speech is actually always a doubling of reality; it discusses "something," it is a repetition, a representation of reality by signs.
Therefore, virtually everything unique, singular in a more profound sense, cannot be related other than in antinomies or para-
doxes; that is, in such a way that this apophantic function negates
or incapacitates itself. This is an indication that we are dealing
with something other than objective communication, representation by an image or by a symbol. We are dealing with an impulse
toward a change of the internal situation, toward a change of experience, toward a new move and look, toward a new orientation.
A dialectic tension between the text and the situation enforces a
change of the interpreter's situation by a regressive motion analogical to what the text expresses. Since, however, the text (or
context) does not contain objective instructions for such a transformation of the situation, but in itself only indirectly enforces it
through a negative apophantic function. There is no unambiguity;
neither in the pragmatic relations— that is, in the acts of experiencing, nor in what they intentionally contain. In fact, we face a similar situation when it comes to comprehending works of art, i.e.
creative art, although here it is a question of a more limited situa-

tion of the so-called "esthetic comprehension." In philosophy, we deal with more fundamental transformations and more comprehensive relationships to being; we face questions concerning advancement to different degrees of consciousness, horizons, and possible modes of being, and, simultaneously, to a clarification of our reflections of all this— and therefore, the study of philosophy and the interpretation of related texts are more difficult.

II

12. As examples of semiotic analysis, I have selected classical and, as far as possible, non-problematic older texts from the tradition on which Western philosophy is founded; namely, the Greek tradition. The non-problematic quality is manifested in the explicitness of translations. This is naturally always relative, because a translation in itself is partially an interpretation; the variation of translations appears in our own language, as any philosophical or other dictionary shows us (by an enumeration of synonyms and homonyms). Polysemy can be substantially reduced by examining the context and perceiving the meaning as generally defined by the tension between context and situation to the extent, of course, that we are able to comprehend the question.

As the first example, I have chosen a sentence from *The Parmenides* (Frag. No. 5): *to gar auto noein estin te kai einai* .... [for it is the same thing that can be thought and that can be] ;[3] translated by Diels: *denn (das Seiende) denken und sein ist dasselbe;*[4] by W. Capelle: *Denn (nur) ein und dasselbe kan gedacht werden und sein;*[5] by E. Cassirer: *Dasselbe ist Denken und Sein.*[6]

13. When we investigate the syntactic side of the semantic analysis, we can see that every translator who is mentioned connects: *to-auto, noein-einai* by means of *estin,* and that the translations in general do not differ greatly, at least at first glance, with respect to the "sense," in spite of the fact that some translators insert words into the sentence which complete the original text, and in so doing focus the interpretation. Let us presume that we now choose the simplest translation, Cassirer's: *it is the same to think and to be,* and investigate foremost, without further interpretation of the

syntactic element in the text that is of consequence in determining the meaning. It is above all the *estin*: here logical syntax distinguishes the following cases which I will illustrate in this way: a) 1 + 1 = 2, b) a crow is black, c) ice is water. The first example implies complete identity and tautology, a statement which can also be reversed; the second example is an "inclusion" of a subclass: the crow— in the class of black things; the third example represents an "identity" with regard to the third thing (the physical substance). Now, which case is applicable to the sentence "it is the same to think and to be"? The word "is" is semantically restricted by the modifier "the same," which would point to the first case, to a complete identity (thinking = being). Let us presume that we accept this interpretation. Is, then, the "meaning" of the sentence unambiguously given? How did Parmenides himself mean it, and what did he mean by it? What did he want to express in this fundamental thesis? Is it meant subjectively (I think = I am), or in an objective sense, as for Hegel; or is it meant in a different way? What did the words "to think" and "to be" mean to Parmenides himself in his specific situation; do we mean something similar by our own words in our particular situation?

14. Neither syntax nor simple lexical semantics helps us here. Therefore we must study the entire context and those passages worded identically and probably of identical meaning and intention. So, we reach for the closest sentence which seems to express identical thought, respectively to clarify the first text. We read in Diels in Frag. 8, verse 34: *t' auton d'estin noein te kai bouneken estin noéma* [The thing that can be thought and that for the sake of which the thought exists is the same.],[7] which Diels translates: *Denken und des Gedankens Ziel ist ein und dasselbe,*[8] earlier on only *ist eins*[9] and explains: *Dasselbe aber ist Denken und des Denken Gegenstand.* Frag. 8 combined with Frag. 5 gives us "being" as the subject of thinking, it coincides with thinking (about that being). A subjectivist's intepretation (approximately as in Descartes) would seem to be eliminated, but the meaning is not fully clear in spite of that. Diels does have grounds for his analysis, for his interpretation is in terms of substance (*einai* = *to on, das*

Seiende). His reasons are supported by the entire text of Parmenides' poem; by his intention to recognize what actually "is" and to assert the impossibility of knowing what "is not." But in order to be able to choose a definite interpretation, we would have to study not only the entire Parmenides poem but also consider other texts to which the poem is directly or indirectly tied; that is, to look at that part of philosophy which might have been known to him. Finally, we would have to try to recognize Parmenides' own intuition by considering an analogous situation and clarify the proper intention of his thought in this way. All these factors will be relevant for our final interpretation of the statement *thinking and being is one* (resp. *to think and to be is the same*). The explicitness of the meaning does not depend solely on the syntax and semantics of the individual words or sentence as a whole, but primarily on the situation.

15. The question then is: What was the meaning of *einai* and *noein* for Parmenides in his particular situation? Furthermore, did he distinguish *einai* and *to on, noéma* and *noein*, being and existence, content and object of thinking? Let us assume that we knew the following about his relationship to his predecessors or to his contemporaries and followers (in the Eleatic school). In his poem, Parmenides responds on the one hand to the teaching of Heraclitus about origin, on the other hand to Anaximander's doctrine about "apeiron," and simultaneously to the teaching of the Pythagoreans who attempted to delimit, to define the unlimitable quantitatively. They applied a more profound concept of existence or being, not only as physical existence in space, but also as substance, as foundation of the physical, which is quantitatively undefinable, which is not "more" here, "less" there (since "being" means either that something "is" or "is not"). Yet this substance — outside of which nothing exists, is delimitable by thinking as thinking is its very own object. Apparently, the question is one of overcoming, or demonstrating the impracticability of the method of "negation" for knowledge, and establishing the basic position before there is any thought of the particularities. Much in the context of the poem and of the historical reality known to us demon-

strate that here we have a case of confrontation with the "unde-limited" and of an identification of an existence with the world of numbers; that is, of the views of Anaximander and the Pythagor-eans, and a higher reality rather than reality originating empirically (Heraclitus). It is obvious that these problems were taken up by the Eleatic school which later, during the time of Zeno and Melissus, tried, in formal terms, to reconcile Parmenides' original intuition about thinking that attains being with the problems of the contin-uum of existence and the discursiveness of concepts, i.e. with the logical problems of mastering the "wholeness" of being which "a powerful necessity keeps in the bonds of the limit that hold it fast." The entire tendency of antinomies or the paradox of this school is to show the unreliability of the opinion of other schools concerning becoming and ceasing to be, being and non-being, change of place, color, shape, etc.

16. It is our intention to indicate here only the possibilities for a certain interpretation and certainly not to select one; we want only to point out that it is necessary to come as close as possible to the situation in which Parmenides created his poem if we are to understand it. It would certainly be a great help if it were feasible to somehow establish various situational possibilities which could simulate historical situations and at the same time establish the forms of thought or expression which are at our disposal. In this way, the arbitrariness of interpretation could be limited to a cer-tain degree and directions for the intuition of an analogous situa-tion could be shown. For that purpose, however, a mere typology of "world views" would not suffice. What we need is an illumina-tion, or a deciphering of the entire "constitution of philosophy." That is an important task which modern philosophy will not be able to bypass. Naturally, this exceeds, even in a limited sketch, the framework and the possibilities of this article. It would estab-lish, for the first time, a really philosophical history of philosophy, that is an interpretation which would not break up the history of philosophy into independent, isolated cases of fortuitous episodes or force it into a definite rational scheme of development, where the following fulfills the preceding as if the preceding existed only

for the sake of the following. Formal developmental links are indicated primarily in the language, that is in the syntactic-semantic
structure of expressive possibilities which are at the disposal of the
unique act of thinking which always wants to master existence a-
new. Precisely this tension in turn affects the development of the
vehicle of expression— language.

17. Another example from Diels's Fragments, from Heraclitus
(Frag. 10, line 22): *synapsies hola kai ouch hola, symferome-
non, diaferomenon, synaidon diaidon, kai ek pantón hen kai ex
henos panta* [Couples are things and things not whole, what is
drawn together and what is drawn asunder, the harmonious and
the discordant. The one is made up of all things, and all things
issue from one.][10] Diels's translation: *Verbindungen sind: Ganzes
und Nichtganzes, Eintracht, Zwietracht, Einklang, Missklang und
aus allem eins und aus einem alles.*[11] Capelle translates similarly,
not supplying the verb;[12] Leisegang also accepts Diels's translation
completely, adding however, that in the case of Heraclitus, it is appropriate to supply the verb *genesthai*, which to him, is identical
with *einai*, as follows from his entire view of transformations, tran-
sitions of existence.[13] Even Heraclitus sometimes uses this verb,
though he sometimes omits it; for example, Frag. 36: *psychéisi
thanatos hydór genesthai, hydati te thanatos gén genesthai, ek gés
de hydór ginetai, ex hydatos de psyché.* [For it is death to the soul
to become water, and death to water to become earth. But water
comes from earth; and from water, soul.][14] Diels translates: *Für
die Seelen ist es Tod zu Wasser zu werden, für das Wasser Tod zur
Erde zu werden. Aus der Erde wird Wasser, aus Wasser Seele.*[15]
Leisegang translates similarly.[16] Frag. 62 then reads: *athanatoi
thnétoi, thnétoi athanatoi, zóntes ton ekeinón thanaton, ton de
ekeinón bion tethneóntes.* [Mortals are immortals and immortals
are mortals, the one living the other's death and dying the other's
life.][17] Both Capelle and Leisegang translate identically: *Unsterbliche sterblich, sterbliche unsterblich, lebend jener Tod, jener
Leben aber sterbend.*[18] Leisegang, however, infers that it is suitable to add *genesthai* here and that it is impossible to translate
"immortals are mortals" since that unity of opposites is obtained

only by transformation in the flux of everything (*panta rei*) in time: consequently, it is incomplete.[19] Heraclitus himself expresses the transition, the transformation of the one into the other, by an explicit edition to the verb *einai*, as we can see for instance in Frag. 88: *tauto t'eni zón kai tethnékos kai to katheudon kai neon kai géraidon. Tade gar metapesonta ekeina estin, kakeina palin metapesonta tauta.* [And it is the same thing in us that is quick and dead, awake and asleep, young and old; the former are shifted and become the latter; the latter in turn are shifted and become the former.][20] Diels translates: *Und es ist immer ein und dasselbe, was in uns wohnt: Lebendes und Totes und das Wache und das Schlafende und Jung und Alt. Wenn es unschlägt, ist dieses jenes und jenes wiederum, wenn es umschlägt, dieses.*[21] Capelle translates: *Ein und dasselbe offenbart sich in den Dingen als Lebendes und Totes, Waches und Schlafendes, Junges und Altes. Denn dieses ist nach seiner Umwandlung jenes, und jenes, wieder verwandelt, dieses.*[22] Here it is not a question of static identity, but one of genesis, perhaps similar to "a caterpillar is a butterfly" when it transforms itself. In contrast, for instance, for Plato "being" is defined in a similar case by the inclusion of a subclass in a class, in which case the classes, or the ideas, do not coalesce. The final question is one of participation in the idea; *metechein* is the meaning proper of *einai*. It is also a question of the division of concepts, not one of transition between things. Here the entire context points to different forms or a different style of thinking, and contributes to the interpretation.

18. The method by which Leisegang obtains his interpretation of texts is worth mentioning. His method is based mainly on the assumption that we do not presume, that we comprehend the text, i.e. that we must first look for the point of view from which we are going to be able to comprehend it. We define it as calling oneself "stupid beforehand," not to interpret the text from our own situation, not to interject our own meaning. Subsequently, it is necessary to estimate the point of departure and the aim, that is, the tendency, and then to attempt an analysis with the help of our own logic if "another logic" cannot be found. By point of depar-

ture Leisegang usually means some kind of image or viewpoint taken from reality to serve as a model for abstract thought. He frequently translates with the help of such a model. This is an interpretation similar to that when we try to explain $a^2 + b^2 = c^2$ graphically by the example of the right angle triangle in Euclidian geometry so that we might comprehend the theorem more easily. In this way, Leisegang achieves various models of thought, various types on which he practices. Finally, he talks about three basic types or forms of thought which make up mutually alien worlds and to which apply, as he puts it, various kinds of logic. Nowadays we would say that these forms are primarily semantic-pragmatic matters and not matters of pure syntax or "logic." As long as it is possible to translate them with the aid of the models, there is apparently a syntax (not descriptive, but abstractly formal) common to them, just as syntax of an algebraic form is common to three forms of geometry. The forms introduced by Leisegang are not complete, however, (paradox and others are lacking) and they are not even sufficiently correctly, that is, completely characterized. For example, the form of mathematical thinking is not just a "pyramid of concepts," i.e. semantic segmentation. Even here, then, newer methods help us clarify relationships; this is not the place, however, to develop analogies between the above-mentioned forms of conceptual and abstract thinking and geometric interpretation (of formal algebra).

19. In conclusion, one can briefly state that philosophical texts are usually polysemic; that is, they allow for more than one interpretation. These interpretations, however, are not arbitrary; they always relate to a particular situation. If we are concerned with the original situation, that is, the one in which the text was intended by the author, then our ability to use our mind in a relevant position is decisive; we must possess the ability to arrive at an analogous situation and through imagination disengage ourselves from the common current, from the, for us, natural situation. We must attempt to think "in the spirit of the age," that is, in the semantic-pragmatic situation of the time in whose background or against which, the text is the expression of an act of thinking of a

particular philosopher. We must not forget that we frequently deal with original creations which generate new concepts of the world, and where, consequently, the thought of the philosopher stands in opposition to the meaning of the collective or against the common or official view of the time. In addition, we have to keep in mind that we are not dealing with a text that constitutes a description of "what is," but an appeal to a concretization in thought, the creation of a new situation, a new view in an analogous situation. When our entire context or the inadequacy of the apophantic functions leads us to a particular act of intuition by means of the concretization of an analogous situation, we obtain an interpretation which can, to a certain extent, render the original train of thought whose tension is reflected in the text. The more abstract, less directionally defined the idea is, the more space there is for other interpretations— even if these are alien to the original, explicit situation. These interpretations may even be mutually exclusive in the same way that the laws about the sum total of the angles of a triangle are according to the semantic function: whether we deal with plane or other geometry. The situation in philosophy is never so simple that an abstraction based on a pragmatic dimension would be possible. In geometry and in science in general, this dimension is not at all important, since it applies to intersubjectively common situations, i.e. to the objects of the spatial-temporal world.

20. What, we may ask, follows from our account for the question of the validity of philosophical theses or systems, in view of the fact that they oppose one another and are, for the most part, mutually exclusive? Moreover, to what extent can semiotics be a test for the truth or the contestability of philosophical knowledge in general? The dispute among philosophical theses does not constitute any proof of their falsity or invalidity, just as the dispute among various kinds of geometry does not negate any of their theses. Obviously, the variance is not only a problem of formal syntax, but a semantic-pragmatic matter. In addition, it is not only the apophantic function of a language, but frequently, whether consciously or unconsciously, a function of an antinomy or that

of a paradox, that is an index of the inadequacy of verbal means of expression for the given situation. Semantic interpretation depends primarily on this situation and on an ability of our operational transfer into an analogous position. It is obvious that many complaints against philosophy for its contradictory views, anarchy of systems, and discrepancies in concepts (which thus were to assert the worthlessness of philosophy as knowledge) really are the responsibility of varying situations and differences in the function of language, i.e. the tension between the regular traditional system of expressive means and the act of thought-modification which creates new situations. Naturally, without semantic-pragmatic relations it is even impossible to teach what an antithesis is(and what it is not); *"a* is *b"* is an antithesis in the sense "thing *a* becomes thing *b*, i.e. transcends into *b.* " It is entirely primitive to judge or condemn philosophy on the basis of a defined, consciously constructed syntax suitable for mathematics and physics and to consider everything that is not correctly expressible in this language to be "nonsense" or an "imaginary problem." The thesis of logic that there is but one language dealing with objects (content language) or with the relationship of signs (logical, formal) is an inadmissible narrowing of the problem of language and thus also of semiotics. The semantic-pragmatic dimension illuminates and defends the possibility and necessity of the polysemy of texts, that is, their interpretation in accordance with a variety of situations (states of consciousness, attitudes, and epistemological acts). This does not imply a defect of philosophy; at most it is a defect of language, for it implies a relative richness of thought compared to the common expressive means and functions of language. Hence, the question of the truthfulness of philosophy is much deeper: it is a question of the range of thought in a particular situation, a question of deciphering its relation to existence. The problem of expressive and communicative possibilities is secondary and formalistic in comparison.

21. We have thus simultaneously answered the second question concerning the role of semiotics in the criticism of philosophy; how can such a thing as a sign, that is, "something that stands for

something else," exist? What are the transcendental conditions of such a function (consciousness) in general? As always, here we can see that philosophy extends beyond the basis of the individual disciplines, however general they may be, into areas where language and semiotics and thus also logic (the formal relations of signs) are actually formed (considered as conditions of possibility, not as the resultant psychological process). Thus, by the problems it encompasses, philosophy transcendentally exceeds the domain of both logic and language, even though philosophy depends on language for the expression of such a (paradoxical) situation. Here, obviously, language only sketches the situation which exceeds its actual possibilities. It delineates the transcending function which then leads to a new situation. This is the reason why it is a difficult problem to express a situation by means of language where philosophy is a transcendentalization into existence itself, be it potential (imaginative) or real, where it is a mode of being, where an individual assumes a position for himself in such a way that he outdistances or outsteps his existing possibilities, creating new ones. Language always strives to objectivize the situation, to pin it down conceptually as far as possible in general terms; that is, by intersubjective means (which is consciousness in general— representable, repeatable). But what if we are dealing with existential movement unique in the full sense, and non-transferable, in a situation that does not have meaning in itself but only for a certain individual by himself at a specific (historical) moment?

Let us consider the example of Socrates: I have in mind his voluntary death. The fact that he drank a cup of poison and did not avoid the judgment of the community cannot have the same particular meaning for any one of us as it did for Socrates himself, even when we understand that he gave an ultimate sense to his entire life by this act. Even when the simple fact tells us more than the whole passage with which Plato embellished this end, we cannot, in fact, place ourselves in such a situation; namely, in his situation. All we have is the external form of this act which we can interpret and evaluate in various ways as the entire course of his life, from Plato to e.g. Nietzsche; that, however, is not all that this act means existentially to him. We allude somehow to this closing act, to the fact that Socrates once and for all, irrevocably and unambiguously, made an existential decision about his life and that the sense of this decision cannot ever be wrested from him. Here the historical event passes through the moment into eternity, becomes atemporal, escaping the objectivity of form (of concept), loses fullness in the face of a living, unique, and complete existential situation; it becomes an "atemporal description" about Socrates' death, a perception of "how it could have happened." The sign of absolute reality is not how that could have happened the way it did, but that it really did happen once and for all and that it happened at all. The answer, however, is and will remain Socrates' secret— his own being. In this way he escaped from us into "eternity"; eternity, however, is not "duration" in time or beyond time (in concept); the deciphering of eternity is— for us— existentially in the "fulfillment of the moment." That moment was Socrates' moment, as it is for every individual; it is not communicable, i.e. transferable by means of language. Silence alone seems to be an adequate expression for something of this sort. It is the "language" of philosophy which comes closest to being and to eternity.

NOTES

1. Partially completed as a lecture delivered at the Prague Linguistic Circle, March 30, 1941 and published in *Slovo a slovesnost*, VII (1941), pp. 180-91.

2. Charles Morris, "Foundation of the Theory of Signs." In: *Foundations of the Unity of Science: Toward an International Encyclopedia of Unified Science*, I, No. 1-10, 3rd printing, ed. Otto Neurath, Rudolf Carnap, and Charles Morris (Chicago—London: The University of Chicago Press, 1971), pp. 77-137.

3. Parmenides, "The Real." Translated by John Burnet. In: *The Portable Viking Greek Reader*, 3rd printing, ed. W. H. Auden (New York: The Viking Press, 1955), p. 78.

4. Hermann Diels, *Fragmente der Vorsokratiker*, I, 3rd edition (Berlin: Weidmannsche Buchhandlung, 1912), p. 152. Both the original Greek text and the German translation are to be found in this work. In the latest, 12th edition (1966), the translation reads as follows: "denn dasselbe ist Denken und Sein." Frag. 5 is here renumbered as Frag. 3.

5. Wilhelm Capelle, *Die Vorsokratiker* (Leipzig: Alfred Kröner Verlag, 1935), p. 165.

6. Ernst Cassirer, "Die Geschichte der antiken Philosophie." In: Max Dessoir, *Die Geschichte der Philosophie* (Berlin: Ullstein, 1925), p. 38.

7. Auden, op. cit., p. 79.

8. Diels, op. cit., p. 157; Diels (1966), p. 238:"Dasselbe istDenken und der Gedanke dass IST ist."

9. Diels (1903), p. 1924: "Denken und des Gedankens Ziel ist eins."

10. Auden, op. cit., p. 73.

11. Diels, op. cit., p. 80 ; Diels (1966), p. 153: "Verbindungen: Ganzes und Nichtganzes, Einträchtiges Zwietrachtiges, Einklang Zwieklang, und aus Allem Eins und aus Einem Alles."

12. Capelle, op. cit., pp. 131-132: "Verbindungen: Ganzes und Nichtganzes, Zusammengehendes und Auseinandergehendes, Einklang und Missklang und aus Allem Eins und aus Einem Alles."

13. Hans Leisegang, *Denkformen* (Berlin and Leipzig: Walter de Gruyter, 1928), p. 62. The translation on p. 61 is: "Verbindungens sind: Ganzes und nicht Ganzes, Eintracht Zwietracht, Einklang Missklang, und aus Allem Eins und aus Einem Alles." The fact that Leisegang's orthography and punctuation differ from Diels's, even here, suggests that both Diels and Leisegang provide their translations with a different interpretative coloring.

14. Auden, op. cit., p. 74.

15. Diels, op. cit., p. 85; Diels (1966), p. 159: "Für Seelen ist es Tod Wasser zu werden, für Wasser aber Tod Erde zu werden. Aus Erde aber wird Wasser und aus Wasser Seele."

16. Leisegang, op. cit., p. 73: "Seelen Tod Wasser werden, Wasser aber Tod Erde Werden, aus Erde aber Wasser wird, aus Wasser aber Seele."

17. Auden, op. cit., p. 74.

18. Capelle, op. cit., p. 133; Leisegang, op. cit., p. 61: "Unsterbliche sterblich, Sterbliche unsterblich; sie leben den Tod jener und sterben das Leben jener."

19. Leisegang, op. cit., p. 62.

20. Auden, op. cit., p. 62.

21. Diels, op. cit., p. 95; Diels (1966), pp. 170-71: "Und es ist immer ein und dasselbe was in uns wohnt (?): Lebendes und Totes und Waches und Schlafendes und Junges und Altes. Denn dieses ist umschlagend jenes und jenes zurüch umschlagend dieses."

22. Capelle, op. cit., p. 133.

THE CONTENT AND LIMITS OF SYNCHRONIC LINGUISTICS[1]

A. V. Isačenko

Our discipline is less than a century and a half old. It originated with the scholastic discipline dealing with language and was handed down from the classical period through the end of the eighteenth century. With the inclusion of new facts in our material, the discovery of new languages, and the accumulation of new information, the range of linguistic problems expanded. The attitude toward the old, respectable pronouncements of classical and medieval linguistics has gradually changed.[2] The way in which linguists of the nineteenth century handled the solidified tradition of their predecessors necessarily depended on this or that philosophical orientation of the scholar. Kant's doctrine of the categories of thought, for example, was reflected in the teaching about grammatical tenses practiced by the language theoreticians of the National Revival.[3] The achievements of psychology and sociology could not remain without a decisive effect on many leading linguists. As language research during the entire nineteenth century was carried out from the point of view of extralinguistic and *a priori* theories, misconceptions concerning the basic and most essential problems originated, and these misconceptions have persisted to this day.

One of the most blatant misunderstandings in the true sense of that word is the discord among linguists as to where morphology ends and syntax begins. For example, Franz Miklosich wrote: "Jener theil der grammatik ..., welcher die bedeutung der wortklassen und der wortformen darzulegen hat, heisst syntax."[4] He has thus included in syntax the domain of the meaning of categories. More recent grammarians, especially the Russians such as Fortunatov or Peškovskij, define morphology as the part of grammar which deals with word connections. These Russian linguists thus approximate John Ries, who maintains that the form and meaning of verbal connections belong in syntax and the meaning of word categories and forms belongs in morphology (*Wortlehre*).[5]

De Saussure holds a very radical view and maintains that, from a linguistic perspective, morphology does not offer an independent subject for inquiry. Traditional morphology (paradigmatic word variation) belongs in syntax.[6]

The basic problems of synchronic linguistics are inherent in this disagreement of linguists. Even though the lay statement "linguistics deals with language" seemingly eliminates any discussion by its obviousness, the history of our discipline shows that no absolute unity exists among linguists; not only concerning the method of linguistic research, but also its contents and its limits. The philosophical starting point of each individual linguist is particularly clear in this disunity.

It is rather natural that, for a long time, attempts toward a separation of language from logic were unsuccessful, specifically attempts to examine language categories independently from the categories of logic. When the categories "subject—predicate" exist both in language and in logic, when we talk about language categories while possibly having the categories of logic in mind, linguistic-logic syncratism is established. A statement such as "a sentence is a judgment expressed by language" is then explained from the position of logic. Such assertions, seemingly superseded long ago, can be found in the work of many modern linguists, e.g. the American Edward Sapir.

Polemics against the presumptive logical perception of language began rather long ago. In his as yet insufficiently appraised theoretical reflections, A. A. Potebňa points out the incorrectness of a linguistics based on logic: "Individual differences between languages cannot be grasped by logical grammar because logical categories imputed for a language do not reflect national differences."[7] In other words, differences in the structure of languages are determined only by a difference in form, not by a difference in logical thinking. Here an *a priori* approach is out of place.

Scholars whose starting point has been psychology, especially Herbart and his psychology of images, do not view language less presumptively. When von der Gabelenz pointed out the differences between the logical and the grammatical subject on the one hand and the psychological subject on the other, the way was opened for a psychological interpretation of language facts. The psychological course of communication, in which the speaker deliberately creates the act of connection between the subject and the predicate, was employed as the basis for this approach. It is true that, according to the interpretation of the image psychologically, the speaker does not operate with language units. His material for the speech act consists of images. This psychological approach has its German representatives, e.g. Hermann Paul; as well as its Russian representatives, e.g. Šachmatov. Šachmatov, true to the psychological principle defines noun, for example, in the following way: "A noun represents that part of speech which evokes an image of the connection between the basic meaningful image (*znamenatel'nogo predstavlenia*) and the grammatical categories of number, gender, case, and of a subjective assessment."[8] The psychological and psychologistic approach *in linguistics* has been overcome very slowly. Baudoin de Courtenay, founder of the scientific domain of phonemes, is still fully rooted in the concept of an image. Even Trubetzkoy but gradually discarded a psychological admixture from his theory of phonemes.

Neither logic nor psychology was able to suggest the correct path for basic questions in linguistics. The problem of the separation of syntax and morphology has remained unsolved.

The art of painting operates with two inseparable elements, form and color. So, too, human language is *sui generis* restricted by two elements. These are the basic elements of language: sentence and word. Not a single language fact can be observed outside these two elements. In the beginning and end of every linguistic analysis, these two elements always occur: word and sentence.

Even this assertion may be considered *a priori*, because we are accustomed to operating with other, smaller units, such as syntagmemes, morphemes, semantemes, and finally phonemes. Is, then, the assertion that every language fact in the analysis is reduced to two elements (word and sentence) not too narrow in a different sense? Where did we leave semantics?

It shows that the known grammatical elements, such as morphemes, semantemes, or phonemes are not independent givens. They merely form a part of a larger totality (be it a word or a sentence) and they then become products of our scientific abstracting analysis. The case of phonology is clear. Even Trubetzkoy emphasized that morphemes are not bearers of meaning, that they are merely signs for the bearers of meaning. Morphemes, even the most productive ones, are not independent units; again, they are merely signs on the bearers of meaning, e.g. *vín/o* [*wine*,Noun], *vín/ný* [*wine*, Adj.], *vín/ko* [diminutive of *víno*], *vín/áreň* [*wine-cellar*], *vín/o/hrad* [*vineyard*], etc. Neither the morpheme *vín* nor the morpheme *-áreň* occurs outside of concrete words. Language utilizes the interplay of these abstract units, but abstractions, not realities, are their corresponding elements in the sphere of meaning.

Many leading linguists are apparently intrigued by the problem of "word—sentence." Sapir perceives word as "one of the smallest, completely satisfying bits of isolated 'meaning', into which a sentence resolves itself."[9] In other words, for Sapir, word, morpheme, semanteme, etc. result in an abstract analysis of sentence. "It cannot be cut into without a disturbance of meaning," Sapir adds.[10] It is characteristic that the problem of "word—sentence" was most clearly and keenly demonstrated by those linguists whose interests have not been limited to the study of Indo-European languages, for the problem of "word—sentence" is quite simple and clear for the inflectional type of languages. It was the Amerindianist E. Sapir and the Turkologist and Japhetologist,[11] I. I. Meščaninov, who devoted most attention to the problem. The question of the independence of a word within a sentence, its autonomy, is one of the central points when we deal with differences among languages. Indeed, without a detailed analysis it is impossible to say how many words the French sentence *qu'est ce que c'est* consists of. Even in inflectional languages which now exhibit a quite distinct tendency toward the analytic (e.g. Slavic languages), it is impossible to determine the limits of a word in every individual case without further analysis. This is also a problem in such analytic processes as Czech *dvakrát* in comparison with Latin *bis*; Russian *samyj lučšij* vs. Latin *optimus*. Are we dealing with one or two words? We are confused by the graphic representation and by the traditional approach, which was cultivated by the grammar of classical languages. I think that the essential question for the typology of languages is to determine the autonomy of the word in a sentence. The problem of word autonomy within a sentence for the typological designation of languages is emphasized by Meščaninov in his *Obščeje jazykoznanie* (Leningrad, 1940). It follows from this that, as he approaches concrete language material, a linguist must first question the autonomy of a word in a sentence and delimit sentence and word functions precisely.

It is impossible to achieve this division by a simple semantic analysis. Sapir's assertion that "the word is one of the smallest completely satisfying bits of isolated 'meaning', into which the sentence resolves itself,"[1][2] touches on one non-essential part of the problem; namely, that the same meaning in different languages is expressed in different ways. The English equivalent for the Slovak word *plaváreň* is *swimming pool*, In German *Schwimmbad*, and in French *piscine*. The same content can then be expressed in different languages in an analytic way as in English, in an agglutinating way as in German, derivationally as in Slovak, or by one word as it is in French. For the Latin *urbi* we have in Slovak *v meste*, in French *dans la ville*. With this example it is quite easy to show the dependence of the Slovak preposition *v* or the French definite article *la*. It follows that the opinion of a linguist with regard to this basic question of the dialectical connection between the word and the sentence has to be subject to a new and penetrating revision in every concrete instance and that further problems can be approached only when the relationship "word—sentence" is satisfactorily solved in every specific case in every concrete language.

Substantive work with language material is considerably impeded by the lack of a satisfactory and generally accepted definition of the sentence. It is well known that many linguists have given up completely on defining a sentence. The definition of word is not any easier. Here, too, a penetrating and detailed analysis is needed.

Only the definitions of both of these basic units— word and sentence— can provide a prerequisite for further constructive work. The definitions of these units are impossible, however, on a general, abstract plane. Every language requires a different definition, especially with respect to word.

Our generation, brought up predominantly on phonological theories, views the sentence as a larger unit, as the sum of certain smaller linguistic units. A linguist brought up on phonological theory views language as a hierarchy of systems: the phonological system represents the base with respect to the other systems; morphonological, morphological, syntactic, lexical, etc. being superior to it. When we remain objective observers of the reality of language, when we do not allow ourselves to be carried away by our analytical concept, we are bound to arrive at a contrary view. In reality, sentence is the smallest organized segment of meaning in a communicative act. The word (and naturally all other results of a linguistic analysis, such as morpheme, semanteme, phoneme) is a more or less theoretical component of an act of communication which is manifested only in a sentence and only by means of a sentence. If we want to add one definition to the existing ones, a definition which combines some currently existing definitions (namely Šachmatov's and Ries's) and which strives to be purely linguistic, let me offer the following provisional definition:

"A sentence is the smallest grammatically organized unit of predication."[13]

There remains the question: which part of grammar should deal with the sentence? Gnerally, it is syntax, but this term is too ambiguous. Syntax often includes not only the scheme of sentence construction, but also instruction about grammatical categories, questions of agreement, and problems concerning declension and word order. In addition, every linguist determines the content of syntax in his own way. Therefore, in the future, abandonment of the term "syntax" for a more explicit one would be desirable.

A further question is whether or not the domain of sentence forms a part of grammar. I think that theories about the sentence can be identified consistently and completely with grammar.

Grammar, as Potebňa formulated it, is a domain of the *forms* of language. When every manifestation of a language form is demonstrated in the sentence, grammar as a domain of language merges with instruction about the sentence. Teaching perceived in this manner further excludes the misunderstandings so frequent for many grammarians. For example, it excludes teaching about larger units, such as paragraphs, chapters, stanzas, etc., for these complex phenomena evidently exceed the framework of sentence and belong in stylistics— this being a domain of language products larger than a sentence. In addition, the discipline hitherto termed morphology, as postulated by de Saussure and referred to by Soviet linguists of Marr's orientation, can also be eliminated. The discipline dealing with the word in a sentence becomes *ipso facto* part of the domain of the sentence.

The concept of utterance frequently occurs in the theoretical work of the Czech and Slovak linguists, a concept which is frequently placed in a certain antithetical position to the concept of sentence. If we intend to preserve one of the basic postulates of structural linguistics— that it is a study of systemic language phenomena alone, I think that we have to exclude the concept of utterance from grammar as non-systemic, as one which does not always demonstrate symptoms of grammatical organization, and because of that, as one which stands outside the problems of *langue*.

What remains is the domain of word in the narrower sense. Objections have often been raised from the side of the Soviet linguists that so-called "saussureanism" cultivates pure formalism and does not sufficiently consider semantics or meaning. In 1928 Marr wrote that: "Indo-European linguistics applies a formal method, concentrates attention on phonetics and morphology, and shifts the lexicon to a secondary position; it is unwilling to consider phenomena of semantics as the domain of word—meaning" (*Jazyk*, p. 128). This reproach of a Soviet linguist refers more to the works of the comparativists, but a rebuke against formalism also resounds in the more recent criticism of both Prague and Copenhagen structuralism pronounced by Soviet linguists.[14] Criticism of an insufficient consideration of semantics is actually unfounded, because structuralism, even in its phonological phase, always operated with meaning as the ultimate criterion for the determination of socially relevant phonic facts. I. I. Meščaninov sharply formulates his demand for the incorporation of lexicology in the "discipline dealing with language" (*učenie o jazyke*). According to his suggestion, lexicology ought to deal with the isolated word and with word combinations of a lexical character.[15] Among the Prague structuralists, the late Professor V. Mathesius, to whom we are grateful for the theory of the designative and relational function of language, was the one who concerned himself most of all with this problem.

It is true that I. I. Meščaninov, in making his demand, speaks explicitly about the "discipline dealing with language" and not about grammar. If we retain this long-employed term and attempt to give it a specific content, we have to admit that lexicology as a discipline dealing with words and word combinations does not belong in grammar, just as that part of morphology traditionally called word-formation does not belong there. Indeed, we designated grammar as a domain of the *forms* of language and not language in and of itself. Grammar then remains but one of the domains of synchronic linguistics and cannot be identified in our comprehension with the "discipline dealing with language."

Ferdinand de Saussure thought that lexicon ought not to be excluded from grammar, even if at first sight it seems that words (as they are represented and registered in a dictionary) are not subject to grammatical inquiry. "A number of relationships," de Saussure reasoned, "can be expressed with the same success by words as well as by grammatical means."[16] The English lexical combination *I used to go*, German *ich pflegte zu gehen*, is expressed in Slovak by a synthetic form *chodieval som*. If grammar considers as part of language only that which is formally expressed, it must be said that Slovak frequentative verbs of the type *chodievat'* have their place in grammar, whereas the forms cited from English and German do not. Any other approach would mean leaning toward *a priori* and the introduction of a logical approach into linguistics, which in the final analysis would mean deduction of meaning from form. Indeed, we know that in every language a logical relationship exists with the meaning "to go often." It is characteristic of the Slovak sentence that it uses a frequentative verb to express this relationship, whereas neither English nor German expresses it by grammatical means.

We have thus arrived at a very important problem in semantics. Indeed, our definition of a sentence tacitly implies "meaning," even when it consciously avoids this word. When we say "the smallest grammatically organized unit of predication," we operate *implicitly* with the terms "meaning" and "sense." Many theoreticians, e.g. K. Bühler and V. Skalička, operate with a distinction between these terms. In the perception of these scholars, a sentence has its "sense"; whereas a word only has a "meaning." I. I. Meščaninov correctly points out that words such as *stolu* [*desk*; gen.—dat. sg.], *stolom* [*desk*; inst. sg.], etc. do not, in fact, have meaning. As a purely communicative unit, one can speak about the meaning of a word only in its relation to the entire predication. We are so used to the "upward" process in linguistic thinking ("from phoneme to sentence") that we completely forget the abstract nature of such terms as "the smallest indivisible segment of 'meaning' "; that is, word, according to Sapir's definition. A contrary, "downward" move is a correct one, e.g. proceeding "from sentence via word, morpheme, and semanteme to phoneme." A word acquires meaning only in a sentence and Potebňa was not far from the truth when he maintained that every word obtains a different meaning in every sentence.

This is valid only when we remain in the sphere of the so-called "interrelational function of language," that is, in the sphere of grammar. It is manifestly evident that "formal" words, such as the prepositions *pod* 'under', *pri* 'at', *o* 'about'; conjunctions *pretože* 'because', *hoci* 'although'; and the model words *len* 'only', *dokonca* 'even' have no "meaning." They only point out the relationships between either the parts of the sentence or the speaker and the predication. It follows that even morphemes are only auxiliary concepts by means of which language operates and expresses certain relationships. In and of themselves in the semantic plane, they are deprived of any reality whatsoever. For example, does the ending -*om* have a meaning? This ending serves only to denote relationships within a sentence and relationships of objective reality. In my opinion, talking about the "meaning" of a grammatical category such as *gender, genitive*, or *verbal aspect*, is unjustified.

It is not my intention here to talk about the concrete problems of the systemic nature of the individual linguistic relationships. My only concern is to delimit the concept of grammar and to determine what all belongs in linguistics and by what methods the individual segments of linguistics can be processed.

When we talk about the content and limits of synchronic linguistics, we have to be aware of the fact that we are merely attempting a delimitation of the operational sphere for the structural description of one language. Linguistics must not be identified with grammar. Grammar is only that segment of synchronic linguistics that deals with the forms of language, and only with those which occur in the predicative function of language. When the smallest unit of a grammatically organized predication is a sentence, the language forms must be examined in relation to the sentence. Thus to grammar also belong the domain of grammatical categories (as long as a grammatical and not a logical datum is understood by this), paradigmatic alternations of words in inflectional languages, analytic grammatical forms, the domain of sentence constituents, and word order (in so far as this is utilized structurally). Naturally, the problems of dependence, agreement, apposition, etc. also belong in grammar. The content of the domain of sentence is an examination of *productive* sentence types. Unproductive sentence types such as *ja nic, ja muzikant*, 'I am not responsible, it's not my fault', or phrases of the German type *gesagtgetan*, 'said and done', do not belong in grammar, but in a special discipline which can be called idiomatics. This discipline would analyze predications which do not exhibit a systemic nature, language artifacts, so to speak. In the same way, none of that which interferes with the regular and unambiguously determinable scheme of predication (whether a descriptive, emotional, or interrogative one) belongs to structural grammar as, for example, word order in poetic language. These phenomena, together with language units which exceed the sentence frame, belong in the sphere of stylistics. Although stylistics also constitutes a linguistic domain, relationships of a systemic nature cannot be readily observed there. In the concrete examination of every language, a principle variance between monologue and dialogue has to be kept in mind. Peterson, who begins his scheme of a language system by contrasting the monologue with the dialogue idiom, also points out this necessity.[17]

Determination of the limits between word and sentence ought to be the first task of every synchronic analysis. This delimitation is an analytical act and that is the reason why the results of this delimitation are more or less a scientific abstraction. What I would call *language structure* follows from the relationship "word—sentence," from the higher or lower degree of autonomy of a word in a sentence.

That part of linguistics which deals with the isolated word in its denominative function belongs in the lexicon. The discipline dealing with the change of words in the synchronic sense, that is, with the change of words resulting from word-building derivational operations, also belongs there. I am convinced that, in the area of the lexicon, we will not find any relationships of a systemic nature which would be other than logical.

As far as phonology is concerned, we are in independent territory. This discipline belongs to that level of language where meaning (that is precisely the area in which we use a system of signs) is only a scientific tool of the researcher. Phonology, even when it belongs in the sphere of research of *langue*, constitutes an independent linguistic discipline which must not be included either in the grammar, lexicon, or stylistics. Moreover, we will have to differentiate between lexical and grammatical phonology (and possibly also stylistic phonology).

An entire complex of phenomena reduced to the relationship "word—sentence" is to be understood under the concept of *language structure*. It is an overall organization of a sentence, or the grammatical organization of a specific language. Questions of the

limits between the word, the sentence, and within the sentence—
the possibilities of a functional utilization of word order, I consider structural questions. For the time being, I see problems of
structure also in the sphere of grammar, as I delimited it above.
The grammatical structure of the entire language manifests itself
in a number of partial *systems*. Therefore, I propose to speak of
the verb *system*, the declensional *system*, and the phonological
system, and to leave the concept of structure for designation of
the overall characterization of the grammatical organization of a
specific language.

Having defined phonology as an independent linguistic discipline
and delimited grammar as that part of language which exhibits the
characteristics of a system, it is necessary to emphasize that synchronic linguistics can ignore neither semantics nor lexicon. It
must be aware, however, that systemic relations do not prevail in
this area, and as a result, the sphere of structural research of a specific language is limited by phonology and by grammar within the
above framework.

NOTES

1. Delivered as a lecture at the Prague Linguistic Circle on December 8,
1947. The published text was revised after discussion in which Havránek,
Horálek, Skalička, Kopeckij, Polák, and Sychra participated. First appeared
as an article in *Slovo a slovesnost* 10.4 (1948).

2. Cf. V. Skalička, "Problém jazykové různosti" [The Problem of Language Diversity], *Slovo a slovesnost* X (1947), pp. 80-95, esp. pp. 83-85; and
D. Kasnelšon, *Kratkin očerk jazykozenija* [A Short Outline of Linguistics],
Leningrad 1941, esp. the chapter "Istoria jazykoznanija" [A Short History
of Linguistics], pp. 52-59.

3. Cf. V. V. Vinogradov, *Russkij jazyk. Grammatičeskoje učenie o slove*
[The Russian Language. Grammatical Discipline on Word]. Učpedgiz 1947,
pp. 539-41.

4. ED. Franz Miklosich, *Vergleichende Grammatik der Slavischen Sprach-
en. Vol. VI. Syntax*, Rpt. of 1st ed. of 1868-74 (Heidelberg: Winter, 1926),
p. 1.

5. ED. John Ries, *Was ist Syntax?*, 2nd ed. rev. (Prague: Taussig and Taussig, 1927).

6. Similarly, S. D. Kacnelson, "Morfologia v celom podležit svedeniju k sintaksisu" [Morphology Wholly Belongs to Syntax], op cit., p. 34.

7. A. A. Potebňa, *Iz zapisok po russkoj grammatike* [From the Sketch of Russian Grammar], I, p. 62.

8. A. A. Šachmatov, *Sintaksis russkogo jazyka* [Syntax of the Russian Language], Leningrad 1925, p. 3.

9. ED. Edward Sapir, *Language* (New York: Harcourt, Brace and Co., 1921), p. 35.

10. ED. Ibid.

11. ED. *japhetic*, derived from one of the sons of Noah. Until 1920, Marr used this term for languages unrelated to either the Semito-Hamitic or Indo-European languages. The term includes all Caucasian languages, Basque, Etruscan, and others. In a broader sense, the term was used for a particular stage in language development, the so-called "third period."

12. ED. See note 9.

13. By the phrase "grammatically organized unit" we understand such a unit as is formally hermetic and corresponds to the rules of the language in question. We also now perceive intonation as a part of grammatical structure. Dr. L. V. Kopeckij made me aware of this in the discussion.

14. Cf. N. S. Čemodanov, *Strukturalizm i sovetskoje jazykoznanie* [Structuralism and Soviet Linguistics], Isvestija Akad. nauk SSSR, Otd. Lit. i. jaz. VI (1947), pp. 115-24.

15. I. I. Meščaninov, *Obščeje jazykoznanie* [General Linguistics], p. 37.

16. F. de Sossjur, *Kurs obščej lingvistiki,* [F. de Saussure: Cours de linguistique générale], p. 130. ED. Isačenko used a Russian translation of the work.

17. ED. Mikhail N. Peterson, *Sintaksis russkogo jazyka* (Moscow, 1930).

SELECT BIBLIOGRAPHY

Auden, Wystan H. Ed. 1935. *The Portable Greek Reader*. New York: The Viking Press.

Capelle, Wilhelm. 1935. *Die Vorsokratiker*. Leipzig: Kröner.

Cassirer, Ernst and Ernst Hoffmann. 1925. Die Geschichte der antiken Philosophie. *Lehrbuch der Philosophie*. Ed. by Max Dessoir. Berlin: Ullstein.

Diels, Hermann. 1912. *Die Fragmente der Vorsokratiker*. 3rd ed. Berlin: Weidmann.

———. 1966. *Die Fragmente der Vorsokratiker*. 12th ed. Ed. by Walther Kranz. Dublin–Zürich: Weidmann.

Funke, Otto. 1974. *Innere Sprachform. Eine Einführung in A. Martys Sprachphilosophie*. Reprint of 1924 edition. (Prager Deutsche Studien, 32.) Hildesheim: Gerstenberg.

Isačenko, Alexander V. Ed. 1950. *Za marxistickú jazykovedu*. (Sborník prejavov v diskusii o sovietskej jazykovede.) Bratislava: Slovenská akademia vied a umeni.

Jungmann, Josef. 1820. *Slowesnost*. Prague: Josefa Fetterlová.

Leisegang, Hans. 1928. *Denkformen*. Berlin–Leipzig: Walter de Gruyter.

Marty, Anton. 1916-1920. *Gesammelte Schriften. 1-3*. Ed. by Josef Eisenmeier, Alfred Kastill, Oskar Kraus. Halle: Niemeyer.

Masaryk, Thomas G. 1887. *Versuch einer concreten Logik*. Vienna: Carl Konegen.

Matejka, Ladislav. Ed. 1976. *Sound, Sign and Meaning. Quinquagenary of the Prague Linguistic Circle*. (Michigan Slavic Contributions, No. 6.) Ann Arbor: Michigan Slavic Publications.

Miklosich, Franz. 1926. *Vergleichende Grammatik der Slavischen Sprachen*. Rpt. of 1st ed. of 1868-1874. Heidelberg: Winter.

Morris, Charles. 1971. Foundations of the Theory of Signs. Vol. I. *Foundations of the Unity of Science. Toward an International Encyclopedia of Unified Science*. Ed. by Otto Neurath, Rudolf Carnap, and Charles Morris. Chicago–London: The University of Chicago Press.

Novák, Arne. 1976. *Czech Literature*. Trans. by Peter Kussi. Ed.

by William E. Harkens. Ann Arbor: Michigan Slavic Publications.

Peterson, Michail N. 1930. *Sintaksis russkogo jazyka.* Moscow: No Publisher Available.

Potebňa, Alexandr A. 1958. *Iz zapisok po russkoj grammatike. 1-3.* Moscow: Gosudarstvenoe učebno-pedagogičeskoje izdatělstvo Ministerstva prosvěščenija RSFSR.

I. [První] sjezd slovanských filologů v Praze, 1929. Bibliografie. 1968. Ed. by Růžena Rejnková. Prague: Slovanská knihovna.

Rieger, Ladislav. 1967. *Algebraic Methods of Mathematical Logic.* Trans. by Michal Basch. Ed. by Miroslav Katěnov. Prague: Academia. New York–London: Academia Press.

Ries, John. 1927. *Was ist Syntax?* 2nd rev. ed. Prague: Taussig and Taussig.

Sapir, Edward. 1921. *Language.* New York: Harcourt, Brace and Co.

SaS = Slovo a slovesnost. Prague 1-9 (1935-1943), 10- (1947-).

Saussure, Ferdinand de. 1959. *Course in General Linguistics.* Trans. by Wade Baskins. New York: Philosophical Library.

Sborník přednášek proslovených na prvém sjezdu čsl. profesorů filosofie, filologie a historie v Praze 3.-7. dubna 1929. 1929. Prague: Unpublished Manuscript.

Šachmatov, Alexej A. 1941. *Sintaksis russkogo jazyka.* 2nd ed. Leningrad: Gosudarstvenoe učebno-pedagogičeskoje izdatělstvo Parkomprosa RSFSR.

Spisok pečatnych rabot akademika I. I. Meščaninova. 1937. Moscow–Leningrad: Akademia nauk.

Stilistik und Soziolinguistik. Beiträge der Prager Schule zur strukturellen Sprachbetrachtung und Spracherziehung. 1971. Collected and introduced by Eduard Benes and Josef Vachek. Trans. by Eduard Benes. (Berichte und Untersuchungen aus der Arbeitsgemeinschaft für Linguistik und für Didaktik der deutschen Sprache und Literatur. Detlef C. Kochan, Ed., Serie A. Berichte.) Berlin: No Publisher Available.

The Soviet Linguistic Controversy. 1951. Trans. from the Soviet Press by John V. Murra, Robert M. Hankin, Fred Holling. New

York: King's Crown Press—Columbia University Press.

Thomas, Lawrence L. 1957. *The Linguistic Theories of N. Ja. Marr*. (University of California Publications in Linguistics, 14.) Berkeley—Los Angeles: University of California Press.

Travaux du Cercle Linguistique de Prague. Prague 1-8 (1929-1939).

Travaux Linguistiques de Prague. Prague—Paris 1- (1964-).

U základů pražské jazykovědné školy. 1970. (Prameny české a slovenské linguistiky. Řada česká, 1.) Prague: Academia.

Vachek, Josef. 1966. *The Linguistic School of Prague*. Bloomington— London: Indiana University Press.

———. 1964. *A Prague School Reader in Linguistics*. Bloomington: Indiana University Press.

Z klasického období pražské školy 1925-1945. 1972. (Prameny české a slovenské linguistiky. Řada česká, 2.) Prague: Academia.